Eardisley,
Its Houses and their Residents

Edited by
Malcolm Mason

With a foreword by
David Gorvett

Descriptions of buildings by Duncan James
Illustrations and map by John Hawes

This book is dedicated to the memory
of the Revd Jennifer Pollock, who
contributed so much to the history of this village.

First published by the Eardisley History Group

July 2005

ISBN 0-9550781-0-5

Set in Baskerville and printed by
St Leonards Press, Corve Street, Ludlow, Shropshire, SY8 1DL

With financial support from the Local Heritage Initiative

Local Heritage *initiative*

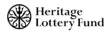

This book is the result of material collected and collated by members of the Eardisley History Group:

Anthony Davis	Brian Jones	John Morris
Jenny Davis	Don Killick	Irene Pearce
Ev Hatcher	Avril Killick	Doris Weale
Angela Hicks	Malcolm Mason	Ann Wood
Bev Hicks	Gill Mazonas	

The surveying of the buildings was carried out by Duncan James of Insight Historic Buildings Research. Dr Ian Tyres of Sheffield University conducted the dendrochronology research. The original drawings and the map are by John Howes.

Acknowledgements

This is the first publication of the Eardisley History Group, and it would not have been possible without the contributions of a great many people over the last two years.

The late Mrs Margaret Hall initially transcribed the manorial records and collected much valuable material on the history of the village. Her meticulous and painstaking research and recording have saved countless hours of work for this project.

A very special debt is due to David Gorvett, who with his usual generosity gave us permission to reproduce some of his work and photographs, and who wrote the foreword. David was instrumental in setting up the History Group, and it is fair to say that much of the history of the village would have been lost had it not been for his single-handed dedication over many years. This work rests on the solid foundation he built.

We would like to offer our sincere thanks to:

The Local Heritage Initiative, for providing the grant aid for the original research and the publication of this book. Particular thanks are due to our adviser Graeme Kidd and project officers Camilla Newton and Jo Weston;

Sue King for proof-reading the text. Any errors that remain are the responsibility of the editor;

the committee and members of the Eardisley WI for permission to reproduce photographs and quote from their scrapbooks;

Briar Cardwell-Like and Ewan Cardwell of the New Strand for their hospitality in hosting our meetings;

all the householders in the village who have allowed us to visit their homes, provided access to deeds and other documents, and stood by patiently while people crawled through their lofts and drilled holes in their walls;

residents, and former residents, of Eardisley, who have been so generous in writing their recollections, providing photographs and archive material, and recording oral histories:

Joyce Banbury	Brian Hales	The Revd Jen Pollock
Lillian Barron	Bill Jones	David Powell
Bill Brierley	Dorothy Joseph	Mary Price
Malcolm Briscoe	Paul King	Glen Probert
Josephine Burgoyne	Sue King	Iris Skyrme
Chris Bysouth	Edgar Langford	Rebecca Stephens
Marion Bysouth	Denis Layton	Reg Thomas
Clive Davies	Norah Nicholas	May Thomas
Muriel Fenton	Gareth Philpotts	Joan Williams

the staff of Hereford Archive Service, in particular the former archivist, Miss Sue Hubbard, and her successor, Ms Elizabeth Semper-O'Keefe, were most generous in their help and encouragement. Thanks are also due to the staff of the Library and Museum Service, and Rebecca Roseff at the Herefordshire Sites and Monuments Record;

Paul Self of the Eardisland Oral History Group, Nick Dinsdale of Lady Hawkins School, Kington, Michele Chapman of Eardisley CE Primary School, Tim Ward, David and Wendy Holton of Moreton on Lugg History Society, and Roger Kitchen of 'Kitchen's Ink', for their help and advice.

FOREWORD

By David Gorvett

Having always lived in modern houses, often as first residents, it was quite a change for Margaret and me in 1981 to decide to settle in a part of England where most of the houses were over a century old, and many two or three hundred years old and more. I suppose we could blame King Offa, the seventh Century King of Mercia, who decided to define his kingdom on the Welsh Marches with an earthwork from near Chepstow on the Severn estuary to Prestatyn on the Irish Sea. The feature has lasted until the present day and, while no longer marking a frontier, it has become a long-distance path for keen walkers. The family took on the challenging footslog in the summer of 1979 and so was introduced to this beautiful part of Britain that we knew not of until then.

With retirement approaching we were keen to find somewhere different to live from the south coast and the Black and White houses of Herefordshire were very attractive, especially one in Eardisley village. We bought the enchanting Cruck House in 1981 and so began my fascination with half-timbered houses, at first with our own home and then with the many others in the village and around. It was soon obvious that history was going to be involved and that the study of the construction of each timber-framed house was essential to its understanding. At that time only one person in this area, Jim Tonkin of Wigmore, was actively working in this field and his continuing enthusiasm and expert knowledge have been an inspiration ever since.

It would be difficult to live for a number of years in an ancient house without coming to appreciate the skill and experience of its original builders, from their choice of site, through the kinds of timber used, right up to the roofing. But, after all these years what remained posed a lot of questions, not least of which were 'How old is this construction?' and 'Was it always like this?'. As the original builders used no plans and left no statements or bills it has been no use relying on documentary evidence. Careful observation and dating of the styles of timber jointing and decoration have built up an approximate set of periods into which houses could be placed. Now, with dendrochronology and carbon dating, there is a chance of getting closer to the dates of these buildings, and their subsequent history.

However, without financial aid such investigations were beyond the means of individuals and so the help of the Local Heritage Initiative working with village and local people through the village history group has been invaluable. The contribution of Mr Duncan James in particular has been a major part in the publishing of this book and in the advancement of the village's history through its revelations. Not that this is the final chapter for so much unknown still remains to be discovered.

One hopes that the evidence of these pages will clear away some of the myths about the houses – the supposed use of ship's timbers, secret passages between Upper House and The Holme, and some wild guesses at the original layout of the village. There is also that attractive legend that The Great Oak at Welson is mentioned in Domesday. Although it is very old it is scarcely that old, and Domesday just mentions that 'Herdeslege' is in the midst of a certain wood, as one would have understood from its ley (lege) name. Not that these past errors should put the reader off carrying on with the enquiries – these old houses have many more exciting and revealing things to tell us yet.

Aerial view of Eardisley from the south in about 1937

The view of Eardisley in the 1930s shows a village, and a landscape, which had not changed much for centuries. The line of the old tramway is still visible curving past the village and cutting across the old field boundaries. The church and the rectory with its well maintained gardens stand close by the site of the castle, now a farm with extensive outbuildings. Beyond an area of open ground the main part of the village follows the road north, separated from the fields beyond by neat orchards.

Just out of the picture to the south the railway station was a lifeline for agriculture and the source of employment for many. In its day the railway had brought great changes to the village, but in time the village adjusted, as it seems to do to most events.

The view of this working community is timeless, but this was a village on the brink of change. In a few years Americans would arrive to create a giant petrol storage dump, prisoners of war from Italy and Germany would be brought in, and, when they had gone, displaced Poles and Latvians would be housed in their empty barracks.

In the photograph three bungalows have already been completed on 'Jubilee Drive', a name soon forgotten. But the rest would be built over the next few years, and most of them would be sold to newcomers to the village. Many more houses would be built. As transport became easier the car would end the village's self-reliance and isolation; many of the old trades and shops would be lost. The main industry, agriculture, would adapt as fewer people would work directly connected to the land.

This is the recent history, but the question is how did Eardisley become the village we see in the photograph?

Introduction

Eardisley at the turn of the first Millennium must have been a bleak place. In late Saxon times it was *Aegherd's Leah*, later *Cyrdeslea*; a clearing or meadow in a wood. The wood was still the dominant feature by Domesday. In 1086 *Herdeslege* was listed simply as a fortified house, in an area that 'was and is waste'. The site of the fortified house is not known, but it may have been in or close to the site of the later motte and bailey castle.

At the same time the neighbouring settlements of Almeley, Letton, Winforton, Welson and Bollingham were thriving and important agricultural communities. But over the next century this balance changed. It seems that the development of towns at this time was a selective process. While one area was the scene of intense activity and reconstruction, a neighbouring area might be neglected or even abandoned. There is evidence that immigrants were directed into areas that had been given a high priority in the process of redevelopment. The value of a settlement seems to have been related not to the fertility of the soil or a favoured location, but its value as a strategic centre. The main priority of the Norman lords who had emerged as the rulers of this frontier area, such as the de Lacys' who held Eardisley, was to consolidate their power.

As a result Eardisley seemed to develop rapidly over the early part of the 12th century. The motte and bailey castle was first recorded in 1183 and by 1216, at the beginning of the reign of Henry III, it was included in a list of Herefordshire castles.

The small church that is thought to have served the village was substantially altered in around 1200, when the structures forming the south aisle and the nave in the present church were rebuilt. The eastern end of the south aisle may have been a Norman chapel and contains a reminder of this time, a gravestone recording the death of Fitz-John Fiest. The origin of the gravestone is debatable, but it has been suggested that Fitz-John was a German mercenary who died in the 11th century. The font is also of this period. An example of the Kilpeck school of carving in the early to mid 12th century, it was thought to have been commissioned by Ralph de Baskerville (died c. 1148) to atone for the killing of his father-in-law Drogo of Clifford in a dispute over land ownership.

In May 1225 Henry III granted Walter de Baskerville the right to hold a weekly market in the village, and an annual fair to be held on the 22nd July, the feast day of Mary Magdalene. This led to the establishment of Eardisley as a town or urban settlement of some importance, eclipsing neighbouring villages who did not achieve this status until much later. For example, Winforton was granted a market in 1318, Kinnersley in 1357.

With the castle, the church and a market, there must have been a settlement, but no trace of it has been found. It would be reasonable to assume it was in the region of the church and later the castle. Elsewhere in the country markets and fairs certainly existed before the period of recorded grants, and were usually held on a set day once a week, often on a Sunday. These older Sunday markets could be held in and around churchyards, conveniently near the church, ready to trade as people gathered together to worship. During the early 13th century there was a movement against these Sunday markets and against trading in cemeteries.

So the picture we have of Eardisley at the end of the 13th century is of a thriving and important town with a fine church, all defended by a stout castle.

This was not to last. This period of growth was comparatively short-lived, and the town went into decline. It was in the centre of the district in which the Barons' wars of the 1260s were waged. By 1263 the Welsh were in open rebellion and marched into Herefordshire, burning and plundering the castles in Eardisley and Weobley. In 1990 an archaeological recording at Eardisley Castle found tiles, fired clay, and fired clay daub fragments. The layers from which these were recovered were thought to date from this time.

The unrest on the border was not the only problem facing the town, as elsewhere the combination of famine and plague was decimating the population.

A succession of unusually wet summers in the Welsh borderlands led to major crop failures and widespread famine between 1314 and 1317, and in 1321 and 1332 the autumn harvest failed completely. Just as the situation was beginning to improve, additional crop failures struck in 1339 and 1345, causing yet more famine and hardship. Then onto a malnourished and weakened population came The Great Plague.

The Black Death came to Hereford in the autumn of 1348, with a second major outbreak in 1361. The towns of Ludlow, Worcester, Gloucester and Builth were particularly badly affected. As a result of this catastrophic urban population decline many buildings within these towns, and in some cases whole streets, were still empty and in ruin well into the 15th century. A number of medieval market towns in the region were reduced to the size of villages by the ravages of the plague and economic collapse.

But did famine and plague affect Eardisley? Almost certainly, but the evidence is rather contradictory.

There is evidence of decline. The list of Eardisley incumbents suggests some disruption during this century, and the Visitation Return for Eardisley in 1397 suggest a rather unhappy community. But this was also the century in which the church was extensively rebuilt.

The plague may have been the trigger for change. In other places where the town survived, the community was recorded as moving away from the infected heart of the old village. Typically, as in Eardisley, their church stands away from the centre of the present village.

At the turn of the century the Welsh under Owain Glyndwr were again in rebellious mood. In September 1403 Henry IV sent a writ to his surveyor of castles in south wales and the marches to prepare his castles and furnish them with men, victuals and armour. Eardisley was one of the castles ordered prepared, even though by 1374 the castle had already been recorded as ruined.

In 1404, Owain received support from the French, who provided over 2,000 troops. The next year they marched through south Wales and Herefordshire to Worcester, before they were forced to retreat. A force of this size could cause significant damage to any town it passed, but did it pass through Eardisley? The exact route of the invasion and retreat is uncertain, but Eardisley was one of the churches claimed to have been damaged, and the possibility exists that the town was destroyed. The documentary evidence must be treated with caution: it was written by people seeking relief from taxes.

With the failure of this rebellion and the destruction of the old baronage at the end of the Wars of the Roses in 1485, Herefordshire lost its strategic importance. Within fifty years the Reformation and the dissolution of the monasteries had swept away the remaining large land owners in the county. One fifth of the land in Tudor England was sold by the Crown to the rising class of merchants and gentry, families like the Baskervilles of Eardisley.

Elsewhere these families abandoned their castles and developed country houses and estates with the emphasis on the aesthetic use of land rather the practical and economic. The Baskervilles seemed to have developed the landscape but not the house. A map of Herefordshire drawn by Christopher Saxton in 1577 shows a large enclosure to the west of Eardisley denoting it as one of eight deer parks in the county. Even in 1669 Thomas Baskerville could still send to Marshall Brydges 'such venison as my Park affords'.

The Baskervilles would fade away by the end of the 17th century, to be replaced by the Barnesleys and then the Perrys. The latter family expanded their land holdings in the parish throughout the 19th century before they were forced to sell the estate. This public auction on the 17th and 18th of July 1918 was a significant event in the history of the village when many of the farms and nearly 60 of the village houses returned to private ownership. Some residents were able to buy their homes, and others continued with new landlords.

These landowning families were influential locally, but the village was also affected by other more widespread changes, especially changes in transportation. The turnpikes of the 18th century were replaced first by a horse drawn tramway in 1818, and later by the railway in 1857. The railway in particular provided much needed employment, and it also brought new people into the village.

As these national and local changes swept across this village few people thought, or perhaps were able, to document what they meant at the local scale. We are left with many unanswered questions about how and when the village developed and what and who influenced change. We do not know when many of the houses were built and who built them, nor do we know who lived there and what they did for a living. We do not know why the houses were built where they are, and why the village is the shape that it is.

These are some of the questions we set out to answer.

We had to set limits on what we tried to do. The subject is too large and too complex to achieve in one bound; this has to be a first step. We decided to concentrate on the houses within a notional envelope of the village. The study had two main strands. The first was to examine the houses, and date a representative sample by dendrochronology, to try to explain how the village developed. Only the briefest of details of the building analysis is presented here; the full findings will be published later. The second strand used what written evidence is available and the memories of the community to build a picture of the people who lived in, and made, Eardisley.

There are limitations to this approach: we are excluding the wealth of history in buildings in the rest of the parish, and important institutions such as the railway, church and school can not be studied in depth. Hopefully, we can return to these at a later date.

We have tried to be rigorous and base our findings on evidence that can be checked and verified. But there are times when we had to speculate and present theories. Our hope is that these will be challenged. There are still gaps in the record, and these will be examined in the future as there are still many discoveries to be made.

Contents

The Houses

Wharf Bungalow

The story of this house, and the surrounding buildings, really begins in 1810 when a large number of landowners and business people in the Brecon and Hay districts were looking for a cheaper way to carry heavy raw materials such as stone, and particularly coal which was becoming readily available from the South Wales valleys. Following public meetings in Brecon £47,000 was raised, and the Kington Tram Road Company was formed. A solicitor, James Spencer of Hay, was appointed Company Secretary. He immediately set about obtaining an Act of Parliament to build the tramway.

The Hay Tramway arrived in Eardisley on December 20th 1818 and to celebrate this event coal was given free to the poor. The line ended temporarily in the area to the north of the church where today there is a wider carriageway. By 1820 the line had been extended to Kington and similar celebrations took place there on its arrival. The price of coal at Eardisley dropped to £1 a ton (£55), about half of what it had been. Coal was carried at a charge of 3 pence a ton-mile throughout most of the period that the tramway was operating. Modest profits were made and in the best period of 1830-45 it occasionally paid a dividend as high as 3½%.

The 'Old Tram Road' did a good job for over 40 years, bringing increased economic activity to a remote rural area. It was instrumental in the creation of the foundry and nail-making business in Kington which could not have existed without the supplies of coal and iron which the Tramway brought. However its death-knell sounded when the Kington to Leominster Railway opened in 1857. Soon after that, in 1860, the Hereford, Hay and Brecon Railway Company bought out the Hay Tramway and the section from Eardisley to Kington was bought up by the Kington and Eardisley Railway Company in 1862. They offered the Tramway shareholders £60 of Railway Company shares or £45 in cash for every £100 of Tramway shares.

The Kington Tram Road Company built the Wharf building in Eardisley in 1828 to administer the weighing of trams of coal or stone and provide an area where trains could be made up and tolls paid. The tramway track made a complete circle behind the Wharf to allow wagons to be off-loaded. The cost of the building was £244.9s.4d. (about £15,000 today). Some extra stables cost another £41.12s.0d (£2,500).

There was a requirement that the Tramway should be shut off by gates during the hours of darkness, and there is a note in the Company's books for 1828 recording that the clerk at Eardisley was to be admonished for his tardy opening of the gates at the beginning of the working day. (From an article by David Gorvett).

The last 'Wharfinger' to live in the cottage was John Lloyd, and his death in 1859 coincided with the closure of the tramway. His widow continued to live there briefly and kept it as a public house. Behind the cottage stood two large sheds containing large forges used by blacksmiths to repair the tram 'tubs'. The buildings were used later by Walter Howells, the builder, as a store.

After 1861 the cottage was let to a succession of Railway workers until it was sold in the 1918 Estate Sale as part of Castle Farm. In 1990 pieces of curved track were found in the orchard behind the Wharf.

I was married in the Catholic church in Weobley. We had Mr Hales' taxi with white ribbons. My husband was a local man; he lived in the Wharf Bungalow. In fact he was born there, his family came to Eardisley to work on the railway, and his grandfather married a local girl, from Almeley. They lived at what is now Dray Cottage, which is where my father-in-law was born and bought up. His father was Alfred Nicholas who worked on the railway, at the station, as did two of his sons, one was a guard and one a signalman, my husband's uncles.

NORAH NICHOLAS

Wharf Cottage

This house was in the yard behind the bungalow and was a two-up, two-down stone and brick house probably built by the Tram Road Company to house its workers.

From about 1870 it was occupied by railway workers. One family, the Verrils, lived there for over 30 years. Ann Verril lived in the cottage into her 80s. She was there at the time of the Estate Sale in 1918, paying less than £5 per year rent.

When I was young the wharf had a great timber yard there, we had a cottage in the yard. Where the house is now there was a cottage immediately behind that, but the cottage has gone; they've changed the layout of the road, the yard came in-between the house and the garden.

My dad, Dick Brookes, lived at the Wharf Cottage with his wife, one son and two daughters. He ran a coal business from there, first as an agent for the South Wales Coal Company,

1

then as his own business. The coal came in trucks to Eardisley Station, and we delivered to Winforton, Kinnersley, Letton as well as Eardisley. In the 1930s this was by horse and cart. Later in the 1940s he bought a larger lorry and when his son Ernie went into partnership with him they hauled much further afield. He was a founder member of the British Legion.

During the war mum and dad had a pig, all had pigs in the 1920s, every house had pigs and chickens, and we certainly did. Dad always used to buy two pigs, when one was getting ready he'd sell the other one and concentrate on the one. It was fed on scraps and meal. Everything was boiled, maybe twice a week, always after washing. The fire would go down low and then it would be a scramble to get the soapsuds out and water put in quick, before it cracked in the heat. You had a bucket of water ready as soon as the soapsuds were out... We carried all the water from the brook or the pump. There wasn't a tap. In Mum and Dad's day there was a pump by the Wharf, we had to carry to the cottage.

Everything was 'down the garden', that was the place if you wanted to go to the loo. We had to cross the yard at the Wharf, the house was there then, the yard, and then the garden with sheds and the lavatory as they call it were all in there, so you had to go across the yard... there was no privacy, but they didn't bother, no more than you would queue to go to the toilet in town. You don't think of it.

DOROTHY JOSEPH

The premises at the Wharf were sold in 1972 to Mr Wadley who later took a partner and traded as "Wilden Construction". In 1974 he demolished the little cottage which had previously housed one of Mr. Howells workmen and built a new house on the same site. Later that year he sold the business to a local man, Mr Roland Payne, (son in law of Dick Brookes) who ran it as North Hereford Fabrication specialising in ornamental iron work, farm and industrial buildings.

Richard (Dick) Brookes

The Old Rectory

The majority of this two-storey brick house was built in the mid to late 19th century. There are also significant 18th century phases. However, the earliest part of the building is probably the timber-framed bay in the south-east corner. Here the framing, which is hidden by stucco on the exterior and plaster on the inside walls, may be of 17th century date or earlier.

It is clear that the house has developed to the west and north from this early core and the roof gives many clues to the sequence. Over the earliest part of the building the roof is made with re-used timber from an earlier building. Much of it is smoke blackened, suggesting that it may have come from a medieval open hall, although it is impossible to say whether or not this is from a building that stood on the site of the present house.

The building was extensively altered when the Perry-Herricks restored the church in 1863.

There is no record of when this house became the rectory. For most of the 18th century the clergy of the village lived in either Eardisley House or the White House. The incumbent at the end of this period was a Samuel Smith, vicar from 1793. He does not appear to have been too active in the parish; he did not sign the parish register once – preferring to leave such matters to his curates. He is not recorded as living in

Eardisley rectory in about 1890

the village, but he may have owned and let this house.

The Revd Rice Price came to the parish in 1815 as a curate. In 1830 he was living in part of 1–3 Church Road, but by 1841 he had moved to The Rectory, which was owned by the Revd Francis Smith. Price became vicar in 1845, and this is the start of the documented use of the house as a rectory.

When Revd Price died in 1859, Henry Cleland and William St. Leger Allworth each held the living briefly until the appointment of the Revd Charles Samuel Palmer, MA in 1866.

Canon Palmer who was vicar from 1866 to 1904 during the time of the Perry-Herricks at the Park. Some of the older villagers used to say that the canon and his wife 'kept the peace' between the Perry-Herricks and their tenants during the times of rural unrest in the 1870s and 1880s.

DAVID GORVETT

Canon Palmer and Sophia Perry-Herrick shared a passionate interest in the temperance movement. Canon Palmer founded a local branch of the Church of England Temperance Movement in the 1880s, and was active in organising meetings, speakers and outings for the next twenty years.

The establishment of the Temperance Refreshment House in the village arose from a request from Mrs Perry-Herrick to the Educational Institute in 1880. (See The Nook). The chairman reported to the committee that as the Entrance room would be made into public refreshment room, Mrs Perry-Herrick had offered to erect a reading room adjoining the club room at her own expense. However her objection to drink did not prevent her from owning the Tram Inn and collecting rents from her tenant.

A letter received by the Chairman from Mrs Herrick objecting to having drink on the ground. Mr Bishop proposed that we comply with Mrs Herrick's wish. This was seconded by General Hore and carried. It was also agreed to pay Mrs Waring her expenses (1/-) for getting the licence for selling on the ground as arranged by the committee.

MINUTES OF GENERAL COMMITTEE ORGANISING
CELEBRATIONS FOR THE CORONATION, 1911

In 1913 when Mrs Perry-Herrick arranged property into a trust fund, Canon Palmer's son-in-l Charles Christie, was one of the trustees.

The diarist the Revd Francis Kilvert of Clyro, was a frequent visitor to the Palmers.

The passing of the canon in 1921 was certainly widely mourned in the parish. In July 1921 the parish magazine announced:

It has now been decided that this memorial shall take the form of Altar Rail carved in oak and placed on the first step beyond the Choir, so that the Sanctuary will have increased depth and added dignity. This involves an Axminster pile rug, 16 ft. x 4½ ft, to match the present one, and if anyone will offer to work four kneelers each 4 ft. long, they will greatly add to the comfort of communicants. The other part of the memorial to the late well-beloved Rector will be the list of Incumbents carved in oak and put up near the main entrance.

The final work was completed in 1922. The accounts published in early 1923 showed that 115 subscribers had contributed a total of £l44.17s.6d. to the appeal. In terms of today's money this would be worth well over £7,000. Considering that the subject of the memorial ceased to be Vicar of Eardisley nearly 20 years before and that there had been two other incumbents in between, one can only be impressed by the continuing wish of the parishioners to remember Canon Palmer. As the parish magazine of February 1923 put it: 'We feel that within the Parish Church is

Canon Charles Samuel Palmer and Ellen Palmer on their Golden Wedding Anniversary.
Back, l to r, daughter Margaret Eleanor and husband Charles Henry Fehler Christie (m. 1891). Daughter Mabel Jane and husband Richard Crawshay Bailey (m. Eardisley 1881).
Middle: left - Fitzgerald 'Burt' Bailey, later headmaster of Liverpool High School. Right - Charles Bailey.
Between Mr and Mrs Palmer, above, Alexander Henry Christie, below John Traill Christie, later headteacher of Repton and Westminster, Principal Jesus College, Oxford.
Front Arthur James Christie, Charles Perowne Christie (father of Lady Young).

3

a fitting mark of the affection in which Canon Palmer was held by parishioners, relatives and friends.'

During the Second World War some of the rectory outbuildings were requisitioned for storage; later they would be used by the Revd Griffiths when he set up a scout troop in the village. In 1956 the rectory was divided into two houses, the larger one for the rector and the smaller one to let. The whole property was sold by the Church Commissioners when the Revd Wilford retired in the early 1980s.

3 Castle House (Castle Farm)

This brick house, of two storeys with attic rooms, stands immediately east of the castle mound. It is almost square in plan and the walls are set on a stone plinth with moulded capping. The pattern of windows and door on the front elevation is, in itself, symmetrical but it is positioned slightly off centre on the façade. The windows, which originally had wooden mullions and transoms, are set almost flush with the brickwork. The lintels are flat arches of gauged brick. There is a three-brick wide string course above the ground floor windows and a two-brick string course above the first floor windows. The walls use long, thin, handmade bricks laid in English Bond. The front door has a shell hood supported by scroll brackets incorporating daisy motifs – a feature that is repeated at the corners of the door surround. There is a fine late 17th century staircase with turned balusters.

A later, stone and brick building, probably 19th century, stands to the rear of the main block. On stylistic evidence the house was not built as a farmhouse. It dates to the late 17th century, c.1670–80.

Alongside the main house is a two-storey brick building also of late 17th century date. It is L-shaped in plan and incorporates much reused timber in the roof structure and partitions, although the brickwork and plinth capping are identical with those in the house. A principal feature is the large chimney stack on the north side. The building is likely to have served a domestic function as a dairy, bake house and kitchen, since the main house appears to have been built without accommodation for these essential services.

The castle that stood on this site was the main residence of the lord of the manor. At Domesday the village was held by de Lacy, but the family do not appear to have held Eardisley for any length of time. Possession passed to the Baskervilles, who became the demesne lords of Eardisley in 1251, when Humphrey de Bohun, Earl of Hereford, and his wife Eleanor, granted the manor of Eardisley to Walter de Baskerville. For the next 400 years the history of the parish is closely bound up with that of this Norman family.

The castle was probably the chief residence of the Baskervilles in 1272. The history of this family has been well documented, and need not be repeated in detail here. The family had two members of great note: Sir John, who as a boy fought for the king at Agincourt, and James, who was one of three Herefordshire heroes made Knight Banneret by Henry VII after the battle of Stoke in 1487.

Little is known of the direct influence of this family on the village, but as they held the land for so long the fortunes of the village must have been tied to those of the family. For a family of fairly modest means the Baskervilles would have been subject to frequent and heavy fines on their estates in Herefordshire and elsewhere. These, together with the *reliefs* due when minors (of whom they had their fair share) came of age, meant that they often ran up hefty debts. Often these debts could only be paid off by charging their lands and revenue, or by the chance of an advantageous marriage.

The position of the bulk of their lands right on the border with Wales must, in any case, have bred violence and insecurity. But the Baskervilles were essentially opportunists and survivors, and despite 'backing the wrong horse' on several occasions, endured circumstances that would have seen the ruin of other families, to become a stock of respected yeomanry and petty gentry in the 16th and 17th centuries. Other branches of the Baskerville family, however, in Powys, Cheshire, Worcestershire, Wiltshire and Devon, seemed to fare better than those left in Eardisley.

One of these 'strays' was a John Baskerville (1706–1775), and although his claim to be directly descended from the Eardisley Baskervilles is open to debate, his legacy is unquestioned. John was a printer, and until his venturing into this art form there were few variants on the ways that print could appear. He developed a new typeface, called Baskerville, and the book you are reading is set in it.

An archaeological dig at the castle in 1990 found ceramic remains dating mainly from the 12th to the 14th century. It is interesting that none of the pottery appears to be later than 14th century as this suggests that the castle was disused until the 17th or 18th century and yet historical evidence indicates that the castle continued to be inhabited until this period.

This may confirm the impression that the Eardisley Baskervilles had other priorities and the Eardisley estate was not managed for agriculture.

During the Civil War (1642–6) the castle was in the possession of Sir Humphrey Baskerville, a Royalist. The castle was burnt down to the ground, with only one of the gatehouses escaping ruin. A member of the Baskerville family, Sir Thomas, was living in this ruin in 1670 in what has been described as 'comparative poverty'. On his death an inventory was taken of his possessions, and this suggests his poverty was comparative to other gentlemen, not to the general population of the village. As well as foodstuffs, cider and their containers, his property included:

	£	s	d
His Library of Books of all sorts	5	0	0
All the Linnen made and unmade in the Great Trunks.	5	5	6
All other Bedd-linnen and Table-linnen	2	3	4
Three old feather-bedds with ye bolsters	5	6	8
Some very old sear Bedds with ye appurtenances.	2	10	0
Stools, Chairs, Cushions, Carpetts and ye curtains And Valliances belonging to two Bedds.	3	13	4
Two standing Beddsteeds	1	0	0
Some other old Trundle Beddsteeds	0	14	0
All the Brass and Pewter whatsoever.	3	7	6
A Pair of brazen Andirons	0	6	8
Four Spitts, one pair of Cobirons, two frying pans, One small pair of Andirons, one pair of Tongues, One Sway, one Chafer with other small iron things.	0	12	6
Trunks, Chests, Coffers and Boxes	1	6	6
One little old broken Silver Spoon	0	1	6
One Table-Board and his frame in the Great Chamber, One little Table in ye Hall, allso one little one in ye Kitchen And two in ye Dairy House and one very old broken one In Ye Great Lodge.	1	10	0
Five old Cupboards, three Deskes, one Drawer, One Presse.	2	5	5
Three dozen Trenchers	0	5	4
Glasse, bottles, Juggs and all other Trumpery.	0	5	0

Another member of the family lived at the castle after Sir Thomas, and the Parish Register records the burial of Benhail Baskerville in 1684, described as *'Dominus Manerii de Erdisley'* ('Master of the Manor of Eardisley'). Benhail was the last male representative of the Baskerville family to live in the castle, although the last Baskerville by birth to live in the village was probably Phillippa Kent. (See account of Arboyne House.)

The estates passed into the hands of the William Barnesley soon afterwards. Castle House was renovated at about this time. Barnesley did not live at the Castle for long, and soon built a substantial residence for himself at Eardisley Park. Castle House was let with a large holding of land.

William Barnesley was a notorious skinflint. In 1711 the Revd Samuel Hall finally ended a protracted struggle to get him to pay an annual tithe of 6/8d. But Barnesley was industrious, and reputed to be worth more than £100,000. He was a senior Bencher of the Inner Temple, and was still practising law the year before he died in 1736, aged 93. Had he come to Eardisley in his early years, his effect on the village might have been significant and long lasting. In the event he was succeeded by his son, also William, who was not of the same stamp as his father.

William the son married the daughter of Mr Robert Price, of Radnor, without permission of his father who decided to disinherit him. At the same time Mansell Powell, an attorney from Hereford, and Samuel Barnesley from London, who claimed to be related to William, attempted to ingratiate themselves with the father and supplant the son.

In 1735 old Barnesley made an incomplete will in London in which many of the names of beneficiaries were left blank. He brought the will back to Eardisley, but before it was signed he was prostrated by two strokes. In spite of the efforts of a doctor – offered £1,000 by Powell if he could render the old gentleman sufficiently sensible to execute the will – he died before the will could be signed. In the absence of a will the son inherited.

Powell and Barnesley then worked with one Cartwright, a quack doctor, who was able to imitate Barnesley's writing, to forge instruments and a pretended deed of gift. These papers and the discovery of a 'will' sometime later gave Powell possession of the estate. Powell then followed his usual pattern of deriving as much profit from the estate as he could

Later young Barnesley was declared a 'lunatic' and the case became the subject of much litigation, all of it in the favour of the conspirators. This situation might have continued had not Cartwright deserted his wife in favour of a mistress. His wife denounced him as a forger, and the Lord Chancellor ordered a trial of the whole case in the King's Bench before a special jury of Herefordshire gentlemen. On July 18th 1749 they pronounced the deed of gift and the will to be forgeries, and the rightful heir took possession of his father's estates. The conspirators were condemned in costs, but Cartwright paid a higher penalty for his crimes at Tyburn.

The young William Barnesley did not live long to enjoy his estate for long – he died in 1760. His wife Elizabeth died in 1774.

Throughout the 18th century Castle House was the venue for meetings of the Court Leet and Baron of the Manor of Eardisley. These did not always go smoothly. On the 22nd of April 1745 William Protherough caused a disturbance by 'swearing profanely and riotously' at William Houlds, one of the bailiffs. He was prevented from assaulting Houlds by William Bevan, the Constable, and detained. Two of Protherough's friends, John Thomas, blacksmith, and John Reece, a weaver, intervened and secured his release. Protherough was later fined five shillings, and Thomas and Jones one shilling each. The cause of the outburst was probably the inheritance by Williams's brother Samuel of his father's property, Knapp House.

The Manor was purchased by a Dr Pettit, who sold it to James Perry of Wolverhampton in 1783. He bought the Manor of Eardisley with the great tithes, three farms containing 1152 acres and an advowson of the vicarage. The rental at that time, which had 'not been altered in the memory of man,' amounted to £578.

At that sale the castle farm:

consisting if a capital Farm House and all Manner of necessary out-buildings, together with a Water Grist Mill and 455A 28P of Land, Free of Great Tithes, ... [was] ... let to Mr Thomas Harris, who is Tenant at will at the yearly rent of £210 10s 0d.

James Perry died in 1808, aged 77, and his only daughter, Mary, inherited. She had married Thomas Bainbridge Herrick in 1793, and it was her son William who inherited the Herrick estates, and those of his uncle Thomas Perry, in 1852. William Perry died in mysterious circumstances in a shooting accident in 1874 and his widow Sophia became lord of the manor, until her death in 1915. The estates, which were in trust for Sophia, then passed to the Curzon family, who adopted the name Curzon-Herrick in order to qualify for the inheritance.

Throughout the 18th century the Perry-Herricks extended their estate by purchasing farms and cottages as they became available, or from defaulters on loans secured on property. The amount of land they held within Eardisley parish only increased by about 630 acres between 1780 and 1918. It was by purchasing large numbers of houses in Eardisley and land outside the parish that they were able to increase the rental value of the estate from £578 in 1783 (£45,600 today) to £4,500 in 1818 (£137,000 today)

The Perry-Herricks were certainly benefactors. William Perry-Herrick provided land and money for the building of the school in 1857, and paid for the restoration of the church in 1863. Sophia provided the Institute Cottage and a widows' home at nominal rent, and provided the ground for the village hall, and in due course these were donated in trust for the village. The estate renovated cottages and maintained the village. But it could be argued that they only did the minimum expected. They did not build many new houses at a time when there was a demand, nor did they use their influence to innovate in agriculture or industry.

At the estate sale the farm was withdrawn when the bidding stopped at £8,600. It was bought privately by

Castle House in the 1940's

Gideon Spearman. Later, he sold Castle House and most of the farm to Alderman William Davies, but kept the 'Lower Castle' (to the east of the main road). Eventually he sold the Lower Castle to 'Price of Neath'. The Castle House continued in the Davies family until it was sold in the 1990s.

It was tremendous livestock area and during the war my father acted as a grader for beef cattle. Mr William Davies the Castle was a sheep grader, and Mr Bob Wynne the local butcher represented the butchers. I think we were very fortunate to have three men from our village representing the livelihood of the farmers within the county. They had a salary of £3 per day each, irrespective of the number of stock they graded on that day.

DENIS LAYTON

Delivered milk to the sawmills, but that was after Tauber, for 3½ years. Working for Harold Davies at the Castle. I remember Price of Neath coming to the Castle. I did some hedge laying for them, when I took up piece work. They had one of the four Massey combines in the county.

EDGAR LANGFORD

4 The Mill

The Mill is a two-storey stone building with a timber-framed attic storey that may be a later 17th century addition. It was originally designed to house a single pitch-back water wheel driving mill stones for grinding corn, but a second wheel appears to have been added and then subsequently abandoned. Stone built extensions have been made to each end of the mill and a brick mill-house added to the front. A large pond on higher ground behind the building once stored water to power the mill but has now been filled in.

A mill on this site is described in the estate sale of the 1770s. The position of the mill in relation to the castle suggests there may have been an earlier medieval mill on the site, but there is no direct evidence for this.

In 1918 the 'Detached Water Mill to the North of Castle Farm' had three Floors, providing ample storage for Grain, and fitted with two pairs of Stones and other Machinery for Gristing purposes, driven by a 16ft. iron "Undershot" Water Wheel.' There was also another wheel on the barn nearby.

The mill was working in those days. My great grandmother used to take corn down there. She used to glean around the edges where they didn't bother to stook it, then she

would take a sack of corn down, in bits, but it was taken there and milled.

I used to love to go there and see it. The big moat was behind it. We used to go there sometimes from school. I suppose we were wicked really, but you could pull the drag thing up – it was only a board shutter, and the water would go down from the moat that turned the wheel if the motor was started. There was a motor to it, but it also used the water pressure for grinding.

LILLIAN BARRON

The mill was sold by auction in 1930. It had two pairs of stones, and the sale also included the pasture down to the road, the village pound, and a butcher's shop and slaughter house.

Opposite was a roadway which leads up to the Mill Cottage where Mr and Mrs Morgan and their many children including Wilfred, Edgar, Jim, Elsie and Mona lived ... On the left hand side, running most of the way from the road to the cottage, was a timbered barn belonging to Castle Farm, which was farmed by Mr and Mrs Davies, who had a son Harold. Halfway along this barn a covered waterwheel protruded. This was no longer in use, but had powered a grain mill within the barn. The water to turn the waterwheel was provided by diverting water from the moat at Castle Farm.

BILL BRIERLEY

The cast iron wheel on the original mill was taken for scrap early in the Second World War.

Wilf Morgan's Shop

The butcher's shop on the Mill pasture did not last long.

There was a little butcher's shop…and then that closed and Wilf Morgan took it over and he sold cigarettes, sweets, fancy goods, gifts and what have you in that little wooden hut until he went in the army and then his wife took over and she put it together, she really did.

JOSEPHINE BURGOYNE

From 1952 to 1970 there was a little gold mine in the village - at least that was what the local school children thought about it. This was a little hut situated next door to the Telephone Exchange and was known as Morgan's shop to the children and to the grown-ups as "Wilf's". In here Mr. Wilfred Morgan kept court, sold sweets, little gifts and all kinds of haberdashery. Mr. Morgan listened to all the children's troubles and stories but unfortunately he had to give up in 1970 due to ill health. The hut was dismantled and a new house is now built on the site.

W.I. SCRAPBOOK 1977

Wilf Morgans Sweet Shop, now the site of Hadley Rill

Castle Close

Castle Farm, date unknown. The school building is in the background.

Southern Barn shortly before conversion to dwellings in 1965

7

Castle Close – *continued*

There are three ranges of converted barns on this site, the earliest of which appears to be the north-east block, now Nos 5-8 Castle Close. This is a seven-bay, timber-framed range aligned on an east–west axis and set on a stone plinth higher on the north side because of the sloping site.

All three barns were thought to date from the 17th century but tree-ring sampling has revealed that the range that is now 5–8 Castle Close was built using oak that was felled in 1530/31. The conversion to housing has involved inserting a floor, and ceilings at first-floor level now hide the roof structure.

The barns were converted to domestic use in 1965 by John Deacons, Builders, of Kington.

Lower House

Lower House dates from the early 16th century when a substantial, timber-framed hall house was built on the site at some time between 1509 and 1530. This house had a wide, two-storey, two-bay cross wing with a jettied first floor, at the north end of the hall. The timber-framed side wall of this cross wing is still visible along the north side of the house. In later years the roof of the hall was raised and a floor inserted. The house was re-fronted in brick in the 18th century when the gable of the cross wing was also removed. Later additions have been made at the rear of the house. There are indications that the original ground level on this site was considerably lower than it is today.

This property cannot be traced in the manorial record and may always have been a freehold. There are some clues to ownership of this house from the description of the property to the north, which records its neighbours on the Lower House site as William Ralph in 1744, William Lloyd in 1774, Francis Coke in 1827, and Thomas Dykes in 1837. These are probably owners rather than tenants. John Dykes is recorded as the owner in the tithe apportionment, with John Morgan as his tenant. Thomas and John Dykes were father and son.

Remarkably, only three families occupied the house between 1841 and 1918. During the estate sale this was described as a freehold property with two sitting rooms, pantry, three bedrooms, large store house, cellar and paint shop over together with two small orchards and a enclosure of meadowland, let to Mr Samuel Charles Davies at a annual rent of £23 9s. 7d.

Down in the other side of the village the last house. Lower House. Mr Davies was a painter and decorator and his wife was completely blind. Sometimes as a child I used to go down there, either for uncle or for mum, and she would come to the door and her eyes – all you could see was white, it used to frighten me. But I only had to speak and she'd say 'that's Lily, come in, come on in'. She used to knit. She was always knitting socks and if she dropped a stitch she couldn't pick it up herself of course, so she had two lots going at the same time. Muriel Parry who lived up next to the Central Stores, in the stone house, she used to go down to her every evening to see if she needed any stitches picked up.

LILLIAN BARRON

The house was withdrawn at the auction, but sold privately two months later to John Bushell of London. He died in 1919 leaving the property to his children John and Gwendoline. John sold his share to Gwendoline for £250. Gwendoline Legg sold the property to Thomas Morris, a farmer, and Evelyn Morris, both of Three Cocks, for £810 in 1936. Richard Tebb of Ludlow bought the house in 1941. Later that year he also bought the orchard opposite which had belonged to Ellen Baird of the Tram Inn; a stone built cider mill stood facing the road in the northern corner. In 1961 he sold the property to his wife, who remained there three years before selling to Percival Powell. He sold the orchard to Harry and Doug Burgoyne in 1969, who built a garage on the site.

My husband rented the garage behind Mr Sharples' house first. Then had the other one built, where he has the lorries now, but he never ever got an agreement or anything official. When Mr Sharples thought about selling the business, my husband decided he had better protect himself and he bought this one up the village. He bought it from Mr Powell who lived across the road at Lower House. It was an orchard, and so they built the garage and it grew and grew and now it is six businesses.

When he started in the garage I took over the office and they had one employee. Then they took on a second employee and I can remember the debate – could they afford it? would there be enough work to keep him occupied permanently or was it just to be temporary? But it went from strength to strength and ended up with about 40 employees – which seems incredible now.

JOSEPHINE BURGOYNE

They built Burgoyne's garage on an orchard that was there, owned by The Tram, and there used to be a cider press there. in an old barn, and I used to look in on my way to school.

MURIEL FENTON

Lower House in 1918. Opposite is Ellen Baird's Cider House, demolished when the garage was built.

10, 11, 12 Church Road

This range, now forming three separate cottages, was probably built in the 15th century. It is a hall house in which No. 10 occupies the rebuilt service accommodation at the south end; No. 11 is within the central, open hall, and No. 12 has the 'upper' end rooms. Much of the original timber framing survives intact behind a rough-cast exterior, including a double arch-braced collar truss over the once-open, single-storey hall. The roof has been modified by raising the eaves level along the front, which was probably done in the late 17th century when the present floors were inserted. At the north end of the building the original timber framing is still visible.

Identifying this property in the manorial record is not helped by the occupancy of the property as a single, and later as two or three dwellings. There are matches between owners of this and surrounding properties, but too few to be absolutely confident in the identification. There is a match to the property to the south, Lower House, owned by Thomas Dykes in 1837 the property to the north was owned by Richard Coke, but as he owned a number of properties in this block, this is not too reliable an indicator. However, the owner of this property in the Manorial record in the 1840's does match the 'tithe' owner of this property and this was the only property he held in the parish.

Despite difficulties in identifying the site, the sequence of transactions is very easy to follow, as it is one of the houses in the Manorial record which is named. From the earliest entry it is referred to as Willsons or Wilsons House.

In 1742 this house passed from Edward Pugh the father, to Edward Pugh the son. His grandson, Thomas Weale, inherited the house in 1774, before selling it to William Lloyd. William Lloyd's widow, Jane was living in the house when she sold it to Robert Morris of Eardisley, an Innholder, and his wife, Mary, in 1801.

Mary retained a life interest in the property after her husband's death, and gifted the house in 1827 to her daughter Ann, by then married to Samuel Wall of Bromyard, a cabinet maker. Two months later Samuel and Ann mortgaged the property for £100 to William Williams, a farmer of Kington. Mary continued to live there until her death in 1833. The mortgage was redeemed out of the proceeds of the sale to John Symonds for £250, a farmer of the Quebb. The records are a little ambiguous about tenants at this time; they state that the house was now occupied as two dwellings, but seem to describe three sets of tenants: 'one late in occupation of Mary Morris, one in the occupation of Francis East, the other void'.

All other references to the Symonds family in the Record relate to transactions for land and houses outside the village, and there is no further mention of Wilsons House. The property must have been sold to Perry-Herrick estate in the latter half of the century and it became lot 70 in the Estate Sale, let to William Gwatkin, Julia Brooks and William Price, at aggregate rents of £16 per annum.

Next door there was a row of three cottages. Mr Price lived in the first. Miss Brooks and her elderly mother lived in the next. I never saw the mother as she was an invalid and spent the last at least twenty years of her life in bed. Miss Brooks' brother Jack, his wife and son Teddy lived next door. Mrs Brooks was also a sister to Mr Price and when he died the Brooks family moved into his cottage; Mr and Mrs Williams, who were again somehow related then moved into the vacant cottage. Mr Brooks worked on the railway and was followed by the son Teddy. Every Guy Fawkes' Night Teddy Brooks built a large bonfire in the orchard at the bottom of their garden and most of us villagers living near went there to let off our fireworks. Mrs Brooks was an expert at treating boils and sore limbs and always had a supply of herbal cures. Teddy Brooks and his wife Maudie ended up living in the Old Forge Cottage at Kinnersley.

BILL BRIERLEY

Hawthorn Cottage

The cottage and the former post office to the north now form a single house. The two southern bays are timber-framed and probably date to the 17th century. They have been constructed against the south wall of the former post office which is a two-bay structure built in stone and brick, probably replacing a timber-framed building, part of which survives in the rear (west) wall. This early fragment may be a section of wall framing from a cruck building, probably of 15th century date, that stood on the site.

These houses are not recorded in the manorial records. During the 19th century they were occupied as two dwellings; generally the larger cottage to the south was occupied by the families of tradesmen, while the very small cottage to the north housed labourers and later widowed women.

It was as a freehold property in the Estate Sale let to John Brooks and the Revd S. Montgomery Campbell, at an aggregate annual rent of £13 10s. It was bought by Mr Lambert Smith for £230.

My father had been a farming student in his younger days, and had spent some time with relatives on a farm in Canada. When he came out of the war he was rather disabled: he had lost the use of his right hand and was unable to do anything very technical with it; he had also lost a lung. He actually used to help my grandmother and he also used to work as a night watchman down at the camp. After it had been vacated by the Americans there was a lot of equipment there. The camp was where Forest Fencing is now.

He did that for a few years until my grandmother wanted to retire from the post office; that was ideal as he was not in the best of health and he then took over in 1948. My grandmother had the post office from approximately 1915 to 1948 and then my father had it from 1948 to 1964. When my father died my mother did it for 8 years from 1964 to 1972 and then my mother remarried and I came here with my husband and family in 1972 and I ran the post office until 1999, and that was the end of an era.

My grandmother was a very strong, capable lady. She was widowed in America when my father and his brother were just 18 months and 3 years old. She came back to this country and her father set her up in business here (her father was a post master in Hay on Wye, Thomas Wallace) so that she could make a living and bring up her sons, and then in 1918, when the estate sales took place, she bought the post office or what is now called Hawthorn Cottage, and she looked after her son. She did re-marry but not very successfully and had another son. She … looked after the

post office for over 30 years and of course in those days had a lot of staff, and the telephone exchange was here in the early days. It was in what is now the dining room of Hawthorn Cottage. She had two girls behind the counter, because it was the telegraph office and they also ran the telephone exchange, I believe.

I don't remember any of this, but I have been told. She had one postman, Mr Cowdell, who drove the van, and three post ladies who delivered on bicycles in those days, but by the time I came here the mail came every day from Hereford by van and we had three postmen. But in 1975 the sorting was centralised and we lost the delivery from Eardisley and it all went to Kington. So it was quite a business when my grand mother ran the post office, she had five or six staff.

NORAH NICHOLAS

Post Office Staff in the 1940s. Left to right: Mrs James, Mrs A. Tippins, (Wilkin Cottage), Miss Muriel Jones (Mrs M Fenton), Mrs Nelly Smith, Postmistress, Mr Fred Cowdell, Miss Joan Nicholas (Fairview, now Pilgrim Cottage), Miss Leek.

Hawthorn Cottage in the early 1900s

Mrs Smith also had the telephone exchange in her sitting room. Our telephone was fitted with a handle, which had to be wound furiously to let Mrs Smith know that we wished to make a call. Many a time, when my father was anxious to make a call and the turning of the handle had produced no results, I would be sent across the road to tell Mrs Smith that he was waiting. I would normally find her hanging out her washing or talking to someone outside. When I explained my mission I would be told to tell my father that she would ring him as soon as she had finished and when she got back into the house.

BILL BRIERLEY

Post Office 1930s

Mrs Smith was the postmistress and she wanted someone, so she asked me would I like to be trained in the office. I used to go down there Saturday morning and in the school holidays. It was quite a busy office.

The telephone exchange was taken out just before I went there, in 1940. When I went down to head office at Hereford there were six girls all trained by Mrs Smith. Hereford were *always ready to take Mrs Smith's girls. Mrs Smith was a trained post office clerk, she was what they called a SC & T, a Sorting Clerk and Telegraphist was the full name.*

Mrs Smith was a very good teacher, and very helpful to people; if anyone wanted any help she was always there. There were six postmen and one van. The sorting office was at the side. Mail was delivered in the morning from Hereford and collected at midday, and another mail delivery at 1.30 in the afternoon. Then one of the postmen took the mail down to meet the 7 o'clock train at night to Hereford. They don't do the work in the post office they used to. There is no savings bank, no insurance stamps, no money orders, it's all changed. We were open from 9 until 7 with a half day on a Saturday, and 9 until 10.30 on a Sunday. They stopped doing that in the war years.

MURIEL FENTON

Our earliest records show that in 1937 when this was a manual exchange there were 53 subscribers. The manual switchboard was removed from the Post Office some years before and by 1952 the automatic equipment was housed in a brick built exchange at the lower end of the village street. There were then 150 subscribers. By 1965 these had increased to 200 so a new exchange had to be built. This was a wooden building situated behind the existing exchange. At the same time subscriber trunk dialling was introduced. Today there are 460 subscribers and their maintenance is carried out by an engineer who lives at Hay-on-Wye.

WI SCRAPBOOKS 1965 AND 1977

Dairy House

This two-storey house is of three bays (each of similar size) laid parallel to, and on the west side of, the road through the village. The central bay forms the entrance hall with staircase. The rendered façade hides a timber frame of the early 18th century. There are modern additions to the rear and a workshop is built against the north end.

The ground and first floor ceilings have pairs of axial beams that are neatly squared with lightly hacked surfaces to key a plaster finish (now removed). There are no chamfers or stops. The first floor ceiling beams are fitted perhaps 12 inches above wall-plate height.

The low attic has a floor and an original (crude) doorway fitted in the truss between bays 2 & 3 forming a room over bay 3. This may have been sleeping accommodation for a house maid. There may be evidence for the position of the original ladder/stairs.

Some elements of the roof structure are re-used timber.

Transfers of this property are not recorded in the Manorial Record. References in the records for neighbouring properties suggest that during the 18th century it was owned by the Coke family, first Jane and then Francis. In the 19th century it was occupied by the Powell family (see Arboyne House).

In 1918 it was let to Mr David Bailey Powell at an annual rent of £28 10s. He bought it in the Estate Sale for £500.

Opposite these two dwellings was 'Dai Pops', who was another substantial property owner. He had been a successful timber merchant, cart maker and supplier of manufactured timber products. If the weather was fine he would invariably be sitting on the carrier of his Vauxhall (12 x 6) car that was 'on blocks' and often would call us across and with the aid of a penny get us to run for a packet of fags. His daughter, Enid, had started a little dairy, supplying milk around the

village, I guess she had lost her workman to the forces and during the war was assisted by a land girl.

BRIAN JONES

The Powell Family. John Powell (b. 4.3.1837) and wife Mary (b. 10.10.1836)
David Bailey Powell (18.9.1864), Edith Elizabeth Powell (28.2.1866), John Powell (13.2.1868), Mary Jane (10.11.1869), George Powell (13.2.1872), Albert Powell (2.4.1874), Edward Powell (1.10.1876), Margaret Ann (9.1.1880).

Until 1954 milk was brought around the houses from the Castle Farm in a horse and float and Jack the milkman was a very popular figure with all the local children. The milk was carried in churns and measured out at each door into your own jug. Then Jack was mechanised and travelled around in a van but was still the idol of the children who fought to have rides with him and go on the milk round. For a number of years Miss Powell and Miss Brown of Eastview kept cows and Miss Brown delivered milk with a carrier on a bicycle. In 1963 these cows were sold and since then Miss Brown has bought milk from a wholesaler and delivers milk, cream, eggs, and squash daily but she has discarded the bicycle for a modern estate car.

WI SCRAPBOOK 1965

Wharf Cottage

The Old Rectory

Castle House

	The Wharf	Wharf Cottage	The Old Rectory	Castle House
1841 CENSUS	(Demolished) No record found	John Lloyd, 40, Wharfinger Sarah Lloyd, 30 John Lloyd, 15; Theresa Lloyd, 9; William Lloyd, 5; Mary Lloyd, 5; Eliza Lloyd, 1 Esther Morris, 15, Servant	Rice Price, 50, Clergyman Eliza Price, 40 Emma Price, 15; Ann Price, 15; Charles Price, 15; Mary Price, 13; Jane Price, 11; William Price, 8; Jessy Price, 6; Servants; Thomas Price, 15; Martha Probert, 20; Mary Jones, 15; Ann Smyth, 20	Sarah Tompkins, 60, Farmer Servant: Mary Lewis, 25; Jane Watkins, 15 James Prichard, 40, Agricultural Labourer Edward Morgan, 55, Miller Servant: James Nichols, 15; William Davis, 14
①		Kington Tram Rd. Co.	Revd Francis Smith	Thomas Perry
②			Revd Rice Price	Thomas Williams
1851 CENSUS	No record found	John Lloyd, 53, Wharfinger Sarah Lloyd, 38, Theresa Maria Lloyd, 19, Milliner William Lloyd, 14, Coal Haulier Mary Lloyd, 12; Eliza Lloyd, 10; Jane Lloyd, 6; Sarah Lloyd, 4; Matilda Lloyd, 13, Scholars	Rice Price, 60, Vicar of Eardisley Eliza Anne Price, 55, Emma Price, 28; Anne Price, 27; Mary Price, 23; Jane Price, 21; Jessy Price, 16; Elizabeth Lawrence, niece, 12, Scholar at home Mary Jane Southwell, 25, Governess Elizabeth Lewis, 17, House maid Elizabeth Lewis, 35, Cook William Parry, 14, Servant boy	Thomas Williams, 40, Farmer Mary Anne Williams, 35, Thomas Williams, 9; Emily Williams, 3 George Davies, 30; John Watkins, Agricultural labourers Catherine Jones, 25, Dairy maid Mary Evans, 17, House Maid Ann Harris, visitor, 51
1861 CENSUS	Not listed	Sarah Lloyd, widow, 55, Public House Keeper Theresa Hyatt, 28, Dressmaker Jane Lloyd, 16, Sarah Lloyd, 14 John Hyatt, grand daughter, 2	Henry Clelan, 39, Vicar of Eardisley Louisa Frances Clelan, 30 Mary Jenkins, visitor, 30 Mary Ann Tryoney, 24, Cook Mary Toffitt, 22, Parlour maid	Thomas Griffiths, 46, Farmer Eliza Griffiths, 40, Jane Elizabeth Griffiths, 19; Caroline Wilson Griffiths, 16; Thomas Griffiths, 14; Robert Wilson Griffiths, 11; Mary Phillips, 20; Louisa Phillips, 15, House servants William Jones, 20, Shepherd John Duggan, 23, Carter Thomas Saunders, 21, Cow man Edward Williams, 17, Under carter
1871 CENSUS		William Betts, 24, Station Master Anna Betts, 21 Ernest H Betts, 2; Walter L Betts, 3m Jane Tantrum, 12, General Servant	Charles Samuel, Palmer, 40, Vicar of Eardisley Ellen Palmer, 41, Mabel Jane Palmer, 12; Margaret E Palmer, 9. Evelyn Lucy King; niece, 10 Anna White, 28, Governess Anna M Harper, 28, Nurse Mary Williams, 29, Cook Agnes Ann Penney, 23, Housemaid	Thomas, Griffiths, 56, Eliza Griffiths, 50, Thomas Griffiths, 24, Robert W Griffiths, 21, Elizabeth Probert, 19; Mary Price, 17, General Servants Arthur Williams, 27; Albert Tomkins, 15; William Jenkins, 17, Farm Servants Indoor
1881 CENSUS	Charles Williams, 34, Raily Labourer Repairer Jane Williams, 30 Charles Williams, 7, Scholar James Williams, 5; Rose Jane Williams, 2	Isaac Gale, 31, Signalman On Railway Margarett Gale, 36 Mary Ann Gale, Mother, widow, 61	Charles Samuel Palmer, 50, Rector Of Eardisley Ellen Palmer, 51 Margt. Eleanor Palmer, 19 Mary Ann Thomas, 29, Cook Domestic Catherine Hooper, 28, House & Parlour maid Ava L. Trott, 20, Lady's Maid Ann Elizabeth Whiting, 15, Kitchen Maid Elizabeth Weaver, Visitor, widow, 70	Thos. Griffiths, 68, Farmer Eliza Griffiths, 61, Robert Wilson Griffiths, 30 Hannah Jones, 44, Domestic Servant Caroline Knight, 21, House Maid Margaret Clark, 21, Dairymaid Samuel Davies, 17; Thomas Griffiths, 16, Farm Servants Indoc
1891 CENSUS	John Verril 62, Railway labourer, Ann Verril, 57 Mary J. Verril, 17; Emily A. Verril, 15; Eunice H. Verril, 10; Agnes S. Verril, 7	William Preen, 38, Railway Signalman Emma Preen, 34 Francis Preen, 8; Amelia Price, 6; Ada Price, 2, Scholar s Gertrude Preen, 10 m	Charles S Palmer, 60, Rector of Eardisley Ellen Palmer, 61; Margaret E Palmer, 29 Mabel Bailey, 32; Grandsons: Charles H Bailey, 8; Richard F Bailey, 7. Visitors: Jessie A Costerton, 63, Penitentiary Worker Clotilde H Alcock, 32 Domestic servants: Francis Penny, 32; Mary Rosa Polly, 32; Elizabeth C Welles, 22; Lydia Hancocks, 21,	Robert W Griffiths, 41, Farmer Ann H Griffiths, 28 Edith M Griffiths, 6; Muriel Griffiths, 3 Percival F Dewar, Visitors: 21, School Master; Edith W Godwin 16 Alice Davies, 17, Domestic servant Charles E Thomas, 15, Farm Servant
1901 CENSUS	John Verril, 72 Retired Railway labourer Ann Verril, 61 Ellen Hale, Nurse child, 14	William Preen, 48 Railway Signalman Emma Preen, 44 Ellen M Preen, 6	Charles S. Palmer, 70 Ellen Palmer, 71 Ellen Douglas, Niece, 41 Jessie Wall, 34, Waiting Maid Elizabeth Pember, 20, Housemaid Annie Watkins, 17, Kitchen Maid	Robert W Griffiths 52, Farmer Ann H Griffiths, 38 Edith M Griffiths, 16; Robert W Griffiths, 7; Vera Griffiths, 1. Thomas W Griffiths; Nephew, 21 Richard Webb, 25, Groom Elizabeth Beavan, 19, General Servant Ellen Thomas, 15, Nurse
③	Ann Verril	William John Thomas	Not in sale	R W Griffiths
④	Philpin	Philpin		Gideon Spearman

① **TITHE OWNER** ② **TITHE TENANT** ③ **1918 SALE** ④ **PURCHASER**

| The Mill | Lower House | 10 | 11 | 12 Church Road |

The Mill	**Lower House**	**10**	**11**	**12 Church Road**
ʃee entry 'Edward Morgan' for Castle House	John Morgans, 35, Agricultural Labourer. Ann Morgans, 40. Ann Morgans, 12; Sarah Morgans, 10. Benjamin Tayler, 40, Tailor. William Jones, 20, Servant. Evan Meredith, 60, Independent. Mary Meredith, 60.	No record found	Evan Meredith, 60, Independent. Mary Meredith, 60.	John Symonds, 60, Independent. Ann Symonds, 65.
ʃhomas Perry	John Dykes	John Symonds	John Symonds	John Symonds
ʃhomas Williams	John Morgan	John Symonds	John Symonds	John Symonds
ʃlo record found	John Morgan, 50, Coal Merchant and cider shop keeper. Ann Morgan, 51, Huckster. Ann Morgan, 21, Milner. Mary A Llewellyn, visitor, 20, Charwoman. Edward Morris, boarder, 27; John Williams, 28, Agricultural labourers. Jane Williams, 23, Laundress.	Richard Langford, 39, Journeyman Mason. Frances Langford, 35, Milliner. William Langford, 10, Scholar. Arthur Langford, 2.	Martha Llewellyn, 28, Tailor's wife. Phillip Llewellyn, 5; Richard, Llewellyn, 3, Scholars. Isabel Llewellyn, 12m. James Morris, servant, 27, tailor Journeyman. Mary James, visitor, 55, Charwoman.	John Pugh, 41, Agricultural labourer. Jane Powell, step daughter, 18, Laundress. John Pugh, 11; Ann, Pugh, 10; William, Pugh, 6, Scholar.
ʃames Duggan, 72, Miller. ʃarriet Duggan, 60. ʃarah Duggan, 26. ʃohn Duggan, 24; Thomas Duggan, 19, Miller ʃohn Pugh, 22, Carter.	William Page, 47, Plumber and glazier. Mary Page, 44. Mary Agnes Page, 17; William Page, 18; Isabella Page, 6, Scholar Jessie Page, 3 Sarah Phillips, 17, House servant.	Mary James, widow, 66. William James, 33, Agricultural labourer. Benjamin Tyler, widower, 61, Tailor. Hannah East, widow, 78.	Edward, Woodhouse, 22, Spade tree maker. Harriet, Woodhouse, 21.	James Saunders, 47, Agricultural labourer. Mary Saunders, 46. Elizabeth Saunders, 13; Sarah Saunders, 13, Scholars.
ʃnoccupied	William Page, 57, Painter and Glazier. Mary Page, 53. Jessie Page, 12, Scholar. Mary Page, niece, 21, visitor.	William Price, 30, Labourer. Mary Ann Price, 28. Arthur Price, 3; William Price, 10m. Mary Davies, widow, 53. Mary Ann Davies, 13, Scholar.	John Jones, 55, Cordwainer. Elizabeth Jones, 47. William Jones, 24, Postman. Elizabeth Jones, 15, Dressmaker. Jane Jones, 9, Scholar. Lodgers: James Edwards, , 18, Railway Booking Clerk, James Elcox, 21, Postman.	Henry Cottrell, 35, Gardener and Groom. Annie Cottrell, 30, Dressmaker.
ʃWilliam Price, 39, Miller. ʃMary Ann Price, 13; William Price, 11; Sarah Price, 8; George Price, 6; John James Price, 4, Scholars. ʃHarriet A. Price, 2.	William Page, 68, Plumber & Glazier. Mary Page, 63. Mary Laura Jones, Grand daughter, 8, Scholar. Jeremiah H. Edwards, Son In Law, 24, Farmer. Jessie Anne Edwards, 22. George Creswell, Boarder, 16, Apprentice.	William Price, 40, Railway Repairer. Mary Ann Price, 38. Arthur Price, 13; William Price, 10; Annie Price, 5, Scholars. Elizabeth Price, 2.	John Jones, 64, Cordwainer (Boot). Elizabeth Jones, 57. Lodgers: Andrew Edwards, 21. Platelayer, Llewellyn L. Packard, 18, Clerk.	H. W. Smith, 36, Butcher. Ellen Smith, 36. Henry W. Smith, 12; Thomas D. Smith, 10; Hugh J. Smith, 7; Charles Smith, 3; Catherine Ann Smith, 14; Emma E. Smith, 8; Milley M. Smith, 6, Scholars. Ada L. Smith, 11m.
ʃWilliam Jones, 33, Miller. ʃAnnie P Jones, 29. ʃClifford W Jones, 7; Lawrence G Jones, 5, Scholar. ʃEdward H Lomasney, Visitor.	Samuel C Davies, 42, Plumber. Marianne Davies, 38. Samuel C Davies, 3. Jane Howbush, Niece, 46, Visitor. James Foogs, 17, Plumbers Apprentice. Emily Lewis, 14, General Servant.	William Price, 50, Late General labourer. Mary Ann Price, 48. May J Price, 17. John, Price 9; Beatrice Price, 7; Rosa M Price, 5, Scholars.	Elizabeth Jones, widow, 67, Living on own means. Boarders: Mary Ann Price, 9, Scholar; Herbert Tyler, 20, Railway Clerk.	Henry Smith, 45, Butcher. Ellen Smith, 45. Milley M Smith, 15; Charles Smith, 13; Ada L Smith, 10; Hamlet Smith, 9; ? A Smith, 5, Scholars.
ʃWilliam Griffiths, 35, Shepherd on farm. ʃMary Griffiths, 29. ʃWilliam Griffiths, 1; Lily Griffiths, 2.	Samuel C Davies 53 House painter. Mary A Davies, 47. Samuel C Davies, 12. Matilda C Jones, Boarder, 19 Assistant School Teacher.	William Price, 60, Platelayer, Midland Railway. Mary A Price, 58. John Price, 19, Clerk, Midland Railway. Beatrice Price, 17; Rose M Price, 15.	Elizabeth Walters, widow, 86. Jane Morris, widow, 78.	William J Gwatkin, 41 Blacksmith. Elizabeth Gwatkin, 46. Edith S G Gwatkin, 14; Emily G Gwatkin, 12; William T Gwatkin, 10; Mary E Gwatkin, 9; Frances L Gwatkin, 5; Allen J Gwatkin, 3; Elsie B Gwatkin 1.
ʃPart of Castle Farm	Samuel Davies	William Price	Julia Brookes	William Gwatkin
ʃGideon Spearman	Sold privately	Mr Price	Mr Price	Mr Price

Hawthorn Cottage		**Dairy House**	**Oakwood**	

Hawthorn Cottage south	**Hawthorn Cottage** north	**Dairy House**	**Oakwood** south	**Oakwood** north
Hawthorn Cottage south Mary Bengough, 65, Laundress. Thomas Powell, 15, Mason.	John Griffiths, 45, Agricultural Labourer. Ann Griffiths, 55. Celia Griffiths, 10.	Mary Powell, 60, Wheelwright. John Powell, 30. Maria Powell, 30. James Powell, 2; Mary Powell, 11m. Thomas Harris, 15, Wheelwright apprentice.	Thomas Hatton, 60, Butcher. Eliza Hatton, 25. Caroline Hatton, 15.	William Probert, 30, Agricultural Labourer. James Probert, 14. John Bowen, 60, Agricultural Labourer. Maria Price, 55, Nurse.
Revd George Coke.	Revd George Coke.	Revd George Coke.	Thomas Jones	Thomas Jones
Mary Bengough.	John Griffiths.	John Powell.	Thomas Hatton	Margaret Herring
Mary Bengough, 77, Laundress. Grandsons: Thomas Powell, , 24, Journeyman Mason; Francis Jenkins, 18, Mason, labourer. William Cartwright, 77; Elizabeth Cartwright, 75, Paupers on parish relief.	John Griffiths, 58, Agricultural labourer. Celia Griffiths, 23, Housekeeper	John Powell, 42, Wheelwright. Maria Powell, 44, Housewife. James Powell, son, 13; Mary Ann Powell, 11, Scholars. John Griffiths, 20, Apprentice. John Harris, boarder, 60, Invalid.	William Wall, 49, Shoemaker. Mary Wall, 44, Housewife. Mary Wall, 10; Eliza Wall, 8; Thomas Wall, 6; Joseph Wall, 4, Scholars. Henry Wall, 12m.	James Jones, 40, agricultural labourer. Elizabeth Jones, 48, Charwoman. Maria, Price, 69, Pauper on parish relief.
James Jenkins, 56, Mason. Ellen Jenkins, 53, Formerly laundress. Francis Jenkins, 28, Mason. Mary Ann Jenkins, 16. Sophia Jenkins, 14; Henry Jenkins, 11; Ann Jones, niece, 8, Scholars.	George Duggan, 30, Miller. Elizabeth Duggan, 31. Maria Duggan, 8; William Duggan, 5; George Duggan, 3.	George Price, 31, Wheelwright. Eliza, Price, 28. Eliza Jane Price, 1. William Preece, 23, Wheelwright's servant. John Cox, 18, Wheelwright's apprentice. Mary Ann, Jenkins, 14, House servant.	Mary Wall, widow, 56. William Wall, 32; Thomas Wall, son, 15, Agricultural labourers. Henry Wall, 11, Scholar. John Wall, grandson, 4. Francis East, widow, 65, Shoemaker.	Sarah Vaughan, widow, 71. Elizabeth Vaughan, 33, Dressmaker.
James Jenkins, 66, Mason. Ellen Jenkins, 63. Francis Jenkins, 38, Mason. Henry Jenkins, 21, Mason. Mary Ann Jenkins, 26. Sophia Price, Grand daughter, 7. Thomas Powell, nephew, 45, Mason.	Jane Parker, widow, 60. Jemima Watkins, lodger, widow, 60, Charwomen.	George Price, 41, Wheelwright. Eliza Price, 40. Elizabeth J Price, 11; George Price, 9; Tom Price, 5; Eliza E Price, 6; Mary A Price, 3m.	Mary Wall, widow, 67. Thomas James, 28, Railway Porter. Eliza James, 27. Arthur Thomas James, 1. Charles H James, 2m.	William Morgan, 40, Labourer. Elizabeth Morgan, 41, Dressmaker.
Francis Jenkins, 48, Mason. Mary Ann Jenkins, Sister, 36, Laundress. James Stephens, Lodger, 20, Railway Porter. Susan Jones, 47, Wife Of Farm Labourer. Mary Ann Morris, Boarder, 11, Scholar.		Eliza Price, widow, 49. George Price, 19, Coal Merchant. John Price, 17, Grocer. Eliza E. Price, 13. Ernest W. Price, 7, Scholar.	Edward Johnson, 43, Farm Labourer. Mary Johnson, 36. Thomas Johnson, 9; Aron Edward Johnson, 6, Scholars.	Thomas Hales, 24, Farm Labourer. Catherine F. Hales, 22, Eva L. Hales, 3; William Thomas Hales, 1.
Horatio Mackland, 49, Painter. Mary Ann Mackland, 45. Boarders: Henry Price, 7, Scholar, Charles Bourne, 67, General Labourer.	Susannah Jones, Widow, 57, Living on own means.	William, Lewis, 52, Carpenter & wheelwright. Sarah Lewis, 52 . Arthur W Lewis, 27, Wheelwright. Herbert J L Lewis, 22, Carpenter. Annie P Lewis, 20, Domestic servant. Ernest Lewis, 15, Carpenters Apprentice. Richard Lewis, Brother, 54, General Labourer.	Edward Johnson, Widow, 57, Farm labourer. Mary Griffith, Servant, Widow, 66, Housekeeper.	Richard Williams, 46, Agricultural labourer. Elizabeth Williams, 44. Edward Price, Boarder, 11, Scholar. Mary Williams, Grandchild, 3
Stephen Williams, 39, Gardener. Rose Williams, 40. Amy Williams, 12; Elsie H. Williams, 10; Albert S. Williams, 8.	Susannah Jones, widow, 67. Thomas Jones, Boarder, 40 Roadman, labourer.	David B. Powell 36 Timber Merchant. Charlotte E. Powell, 34. Elna M. Powell, 1. Thomas Haynes, 25, Wheelwright.	Unoccupied	John Hughes, widower, 39, Cattleman on farm.
John Brooks.	Revd Montgomery Campbell.	David Bailey Powell.	Thomas Hamar	R W Griffiths
Mr Lambert Smith.		Mr. D. Powell	Mr. Tebb	

14

Tram Inn	**Foxpie Cottage**	**Chapel**	**Chapel House**	**The Firs**

Tram Inn	**Foxpie Cottage** east (Sunfold)	**Foxpie Cottage** west (Cartref)	**Chapel House**	**The Firs**
…r Watkins, 65, Innkeeper. …s Watkins, 25. …ma, Watkins, 6.	Unoccupied		Francis East, 40, Shoemaker. Joanna East, 30. Harriett East, 1m. John Williams, 40. Matilda Downs, 25, Servant.	William Nott, 35, Carpenter. Mary Nott, 30. Edward Davies, 25, Dissenting Minister.
…rd Banks.	Richard Banks.		James Barrett.	James Barrett.
…s Watkins.	William Meredith.		Francis East.	William Nott.

…s Watkins, 35, Victualer.
…beth Watkins, 42.
…d J. Watkins, 5; Alice Watkins,
…cholars.
…beth Tringham, niece, 12,
…olar. John Symonds, uncle, 73,
…tired farmer. Boarders: James
…gh, 43, Mason; Jeremiah
…Conie, 41, Travelling hawker.
	Thomas Davies, 34,
	  Blacksmith.
	Jane Davies, 33.
	Emma Davies, 9; Thomas
	  Davies, 7, Scholars.
	James Crompton, apprentice,
	  13.
	James, Shepherd, boarder, 28,
	  Agricultural labourer.
			Francis East, 55, Shoemaker.
			Joanna East, 40.
			Harriet East, 10, Scholar.
			Hannah Pugh, boarder, 57, Pauper
			  on parish relief.
				William Nott, 45, Carpenter.
				Mary Nott, 41.
				Margaret Lewis, mother in law, 70.

…s Watkins, 48, Inn keeper.
…en Watkins, 40, Inn keepers
…e. Alfred James Watkins, 15,
…ocer. Alice Watkins, 13;
…ederick Watkins, 5, Scholars.
…lliam Watkins, 3; John Tudor
…atkins, 4m. Ann Watkins, 13,
…ouse servant. Charles
…shington, 39, House
…corator.
	James Duggan, 66, Labourer.
	Margaret Duggan, 60.
	William Duggan, 39, Labourer.
		John Jay, 31, Tailor.
		Jane Jay, 27.
		William Francis Jay, 7m.
			Maria Powell, widow, 56,
			  Seamstress.
				William Nott, 57, Carpenter.
				Mary Nott, 53, Seamstress.
				Margaret Lewis, mother in law, widow,
				  80.

…n Watkins, widow, 50, Inn
…eeper.
…e Watkins, Step daughter, 24.
…iam Watkins, 13; John Watkins,
…; Ellen Watkins, 7, Scholars.
…n Watkins, nephew, 26,
…bourer.
	Margaret Duggan, widow, 72.		John Savaker, 53, Saddler.
			Betsy Savaker, 32.
			Anne Savaker, 7; Mary Alice
			  Savaker, 5, Scholars.
			Martha M Savaker, 2; Edith Jane
			  Savaker, 2m.
			Edwin Powell, lodger, 25,
			  Bricklayer.
				John Jay, 41, Tailor and Draper.
				Sarah Jay, 39.
				William J Jay, 10; John Jay, 7; Charlotte
				  E Jay, 4, Scholars.
				Sarah Ann Jay, 2; Ellen Jay, 7m.
				Naomi Knight, Servant, 15, General
				  Servant.
				Charles Gregory, 15, Tailors Apprentice.

…n Watkins, widow, 60, Inn
…eeper.
…e Watkins, 20, Joiner
…n Watkins, 17,
…ph Herriots, Servant, 42,
…bourer (Indoor)
	Ann Fleetwood, widow, 70.
	Lodgers: Richard Roberts, 51,
	  Labourer (General); John
	  Pikes, 36, Railway Labourer;
	  John Watkins, 35, Railway
	  Labourer; Horatio
	  Mackland, 39, Painter.
			John Saveker, 43, Saddler.
			Elizabeth Saveker, 42, Local
			  Methodist Preacher
			  (Missionary).
			Annie E. Saveker, 17; Mary Alice
			  Saveker, 15; Martha Margery
			  Saveker, 12; Edith Jane Saveker,
			  10; Maria Agnes Saveker, 7;
			  Marian Ada Saveker, 4, Scholars.
				John Jay, widow, 51, Tailor & Draper.
				William F. Jay, 20, Schoolmaster.
				John Jay, 17, Tailor.
				Sarah A. Jay, 12; Ellen Jay, 10; Harley T.
				  Jay, 9, Scholars.
				Jane Ross, Boarder, 56, Housekeeper .

…s Baird, 34, Inn Keeper.
…a Baird, 28.
…e Morris, 22; Joseph
…rberts, 53, General Servants.
	Charles Haynes, 53,
	  Shoemaker.
	Ann Haynes, 53, Dressmaker.
	Louisa Haynes, 13, Scholar.
	Henry G. Williams, 15,
	  Apprentice Shoemaker.
			John, Saveker, 53, Saddler.
			Elizabeth Saveker, 53.
			Mary A Saveker, 25, Dressmaker.
			Marian A Saveker, 14.
			Grandsons: Albert Jones, 1;
			  Douglas H Jones, 1 m.
				John Jay, 61, Tailor.
				Ellen Jay, 20, Housekeeper.

…s Baird, 44, Coal merchant
…d publican. Ellen Baird, 37.
…ederick J. Baird, 9. Rhonda
…lburn, 24 House maid. Esther
…rner, 12 General Servant. John
…vies, 28, Groom. Joseph
…rriots, 62 Carter.
	Edward Johnson, 65 General
	  Labourer.
	Sarah Johnson, 55.
		Elizabeth Lloyd, widow, 60,
		  Laundress.
		Thomas Kinsey, Boarder, 24,
		  Journey man Baker.
		George Crockford, visitor, 14,
		  Gardeners boy.
			John Saveker 63 Saddle and Harness
			  maker. Elizabeth Saveker, 62.
			Mary A Saveker, 35. Martha M
			  Saveker, 32 Mistress, Great Oak
			  School. Marian A Saveker, 24
			  Dress Maker. Grandsons: Albert
			  Jones, 11; Douglas H Jones, 10
				Charles Haynes, 63, Boot Maker.
				Charlotte Haynes, 48, Dress Maker.

Ellen Baird	Nurse Worthington	Mrs Elizabeth Lloyd	John Saveker.	Charles Haynes
…Baird	Mr Tebb		Mr. Triffit	Mr. Triffit

Clifton House

Cruck Cottage Rose Cottage Ivy Cottage

	Clifton House	Cruck House	Rose Cottage	Ivy Cottage
1841 CENSUS	Unoccupied.	William Langford, 70, Stonemason. Ann Langford, 60. Mary Morgans, 13.	William Jones, 75, Agricultural Labourer. Mary Jones, 65. Sarah Jones, 14; Charles Jones, 11.	Ivy Cottage John Goods, 30, Tailor. Sarah Goods, 30. Tracy Goods, 5; Bartley Goods, 3; Susan Goods, 1y 6m.
①	Richard Banks.	Martha Powell.	Revd Rice Price.	Revd Rice Price.
②	William Meredith.	William Langford.	William Jones.	James Jenkins.
1851 CENSUS	Susan Perrin, 24, Schoolmistress. Joseph Perrin, son, 4; William Perrin, son, 2, Scholars at home. Mary Bullen, sister, 4.	James Davies, 47, Gardener. Margaret Davies, 84. Charlotte Price, 45, Laundress at home. William Price, 10.	John Tedward, 23, Carpenter. Mary Ann Tedward, 19, Laundress.	James Morris, 60 Agricultural labourer. Hannah Herrin, 50, Housekeeper.
1861 CENSUS	Thomas Weaver, 33, Mason. Eliza Ann Weaver, 21. John Weaver, 1. Susan Turrell, widow, 61.	Thomas Postings, 24, Sawyer. Jane Postings, 36.	No record found.	Thomas East, 45, Shoemaker. Rosanna East, 36. Caroline East, 13; William East, 12; Selina East, 10; Emma Emily East, 8; Richard East, son, 4 Rosanne East, 2.
1871 CENSUS	Thomas Davies, 27, Blacksmith. Mary Ann Davies, 24. Anne Davies, 7m.	Thomas Postings, 35, Labourer. Jane Postings, 46. Jane Page, Mother in law, widow, 77. William Page, nephew, 20, Hawker. Lodgers: John Chance, 46, Labourer. Edward Beavan, 47, Labourer.	Richard Duggan, 70, Agricultural labourer. Ann Duggan, 70. Edward Storker, 66, Agricultural labourer. Martha Storker, 60. William James, lodger, 40, Agricultural labourer.	Thomas East, 55, Shoemaker. Rose Hannah East, 47. Richard East, 14, Shoemaker. Rose Anna East, 12; Albert C East, 5; Arthur E 9; Leonard East, 4, Scholars. Fred Bayliss, 18, Apprentice shoemaker.
1881 CENSUS	Richard Pinches, 30, Spade Tree Maker. Elizabeth Pinches, 33. Jane Pinches, 8; Elizabeth Pinches, 5, Scholars. Richard H. Pinches, 3; William Pinches, 11m.	Thomas Postings, 44, Fruit Dealer. Jane Postings, 56. Joseph Bubb, Lodger, 35, Labourer.	James Taylor, 57, Gardener. Mary Taylor, 60.	Thomas East, 65, Boot & Shoe Maker. Rose Anna East, 58. Richard East, 24, Boot & Shoe Maker. Leonard East, 14, Scholar. George W.T. East, Grandson, 4. Emily East, Grand daughter, 3. Elizabeth E. Richards, Lodger, 22, Certificated School Mistress.
1891 CENSUS	Unoccupied.	William Bailey, 31, Spade Tree Maker. Emma Bailey, 30. Charles Bailey, 10; Olive E Bailey, 8, ? A Bailey, 6, Scholar. Ethel C. Bailey, 4 , Lucy M Bailey, 10m. Jane Postings, 66, Tailoress.	James Taylor, 67, Gardener. Mary Taylor, 70.	Thomas East, 75, Shoe Repairer. Leonard East, 24, Gardener. Susannah East, 75, Housekeeper.
1901 CENSUS	William Hadley 42, Police Constable. Eliza Hadley 37. William T Hadley, 13; Edward G Hadley, 9; Francis M Hadley 2.	William Bailey 41, Spade Tree maker. Emma Bailey 42. Ethel C. Bailey 14; Lucy M Bailey 10; Rose E. Bailey 8; William E Bailey, 6; Jessie G. Bailey 3; Gladys Bailey 1.	Mary Taylor, widow, 80 Living on own means.	Harriet Williams, widow, 55, Living on own means.
③	Charles Coxhall	Mrs Bailey.	William Cartwright.	Reginald Still.
④	Mr. Coxhall	Mr. Tebb.	Mr. Cartwright.	Mr. Cartwright

① **TITHE OWNER**   ② **TITHE TENANT**   ③ **1918 SALE**   ④ **PURCHASER**

Northview   **Fairview**   **Knapp House**

Northview	Knapp House north	Knapp House south
Samuel Phillips, 55, Wheelwright Elizabeth Phillips, 50. Thomas Phillips, 20, Journeyman Wheelwright. Carlos Brown, 15, Wheelwright apprentice.	William Wall, 35, Shoemaker. Mary Wall, 30. William Wall, 10; Ann Wall, 8; Jane Wall, 6; James Wall, 5; Mary Wall, 1. Jane Griffiths, 35, Pauper. Sarah Vaughan, 50, Agricultural labourer.	
Samuel Phillips.	Thomas Phillips.	
Samuel Phillips.	William Wall.	
Samuel Phillips, 65, Wheelwright. Elizabeth Phillips, 60, Agricultural labourer.	Thomas Price, 57. Elizabeth Price, 59. Elizabeth Price, 23. William Weaver, boarder, 18.	Mary Evans, 52, Seamstress.
Samuel Phillips, 47, Wheelwright. Jane Phillips, 44.	John Brookes, 26, Agricultural labourer. Mary Brookes, 25. Edward Brookes, 4; James, Brookes, 1.	
Samuel Phillips, 58, Wheelwright. Jane Phillips, 54. W. Alex Ramsey, lodger, 32, Land Agent. Visitors: L Sagt H Ramsey, 28; James Ramsey, 70, Farmer.	Edwin Gregory, 25, Farm servant. Harriet Gregory, 20. Alice Gregory, 1; Eliza Gregory, 4m.	Alfred Higgins, 37, Farm servant. Elizabeth Higgins, 26. Sarah Ann Higgins, 8, Scholar. William Higgins, 3.
Jane Phillips, widow, 65, No Occupation. Mary Lewis, Sister, 68, No Occupation. Jane Morris, Boarder, widow, 85, No Occupation.	William Davies, 40, Farm Labourer. Fanny Davies, 39. James Davies, 13; George Davies, 10; William Davies, 4; Elizabeth Davies, 7, Scholars Fanny Davies, 2.	
Isobel Page, 37, Dressmaker. Myra P Jones, niece, 15. Boarders: Agnes Bailey, 24, School Teacher. Frederick C Goodall, 9, Scholar.	James Hughes, 41, Agricultural labourer. Selina Hughes, 42. James Hughes, 12; Ellen Hughes, 8; Mary Hughes, 6, Scholars. John Hughes, 3. Visitors: Emma Watkins, 45, living on own means. Kate Watkins, 8; Lizzie Watkins, 6; William Watkins, 5, Scholars. George Alford, boarder, 37, Spade Tree Turner.	William Davies, 23, Agricultural labourer. Alice Davies, 23. William Davies, 4; Elizabeth Davies, 1.
William Tantram 67, Railway Inspector. Jane Tantram 67. Annie Tantram, 26. Marcell Russell, Grandson, 13. Boarders: Esther Brown, 16, Postal Clerk; Robert Pewtress, 22, Railway Signalman.	James Hughes 49 Farm labourer worker. Selina Hughes 50. John Hughes, 13.	Unoccupied.
William Tantram	Not in Sale.	
Mr. Tantram	Not in Sale.	

Northview

Knapp House

Oakwood

English Heritage date this timber-framed house to the late 16th century with mid-19th and mid-20th century alterations. The building had an L-plan, the main range is of one framed bay, aligned north/south with a large chimney. The cross-wing to the south is of three framed bays, with a 20th century wing of two storeys at the centre of the south elevation. The cross-wing gable end has a ground floor 2-light leaded casement, and an original 3-light mullioned on a first floor window. A first floor window on the south side has an original moulded sill.

The history of the occupation of this property is as complex as its construction. It included other buildings in the grounds in the past, but how these buildings relate to each other and how they were occupied is unclear.

The Tithe map shows this property as two plots. The boundary between them appears to divide the present house in two. The smaller plot to the north (Number 739) is described as two tenements, and includes a curious square of land next to the road. To the south of the present house there is another large habitable dwelling set back, identified separately as plot 740. The assumption must be that there were at least three dwellings here.

The sequence of transactions in the manorial records ties it to the descriptions of the surrounding properties and the tithe map, but exactly which parts of the property each transaction applies to and how the property was divided up is not clear.

In the early 1700's the property was owned by John Walker, a blacksmith, and his wife Katherine. John died in 1706, shortly before the birth of his son also John. Katherine married Richard Lawrence in 1715. Richard was a member of a wealthy family in the village, he also owned the neighbouring properties.

Katherine died in 1722. There must have been some problem with the inheritance because although her son John was living in the property, it was not until 1730 that he was formally admitted. This entry mentions a James Walker, as 'having the other part on the north', but he was not formally admitted to this until 1735. Both these properties are described as a *moiety*, that is, a share in a property, usually divided during an inheritance. There is no indication what relationship James had with John, as there is no record of his birth in the parish.

The entry for James is particularly intriguing. The property to the north of John's house is described as 'part of a house and that part thereof once a stable'. Was this stable part of the house, or a separate building to the north, or was it the large building shown on the tithe map?

John Walker mortgaged his part of the house to William Jones in 1732, and they surrendered the property to the Lord of the Manor in 1735. This part of the property is not mentioned again, and subsequent records seem to relate only to the northern part of the house.

James Walker sold his part to Thomas Pugh, a tailor, and his wife Elizabeth in 1737. At the time it was occupied by 'Thomas Davies (on the east), and John West'; the division seemed to be east-west, not north-south as might be expected. Thomas must have established an entail (condition) in his will. Although his son Stephen inherited in 1749, his sister, Ann Langford, replaced John West as a tenant, and it was Ann who inherited in 1767, as daughter and heir of Thomas Pugh.

Richard and Ann Langford mortgaged the house to John Evans for £90 in 1775. This was repaid by 1795 by their son Richard Langford. In turn, his son Richard – of Staunton on Wye – inherited the house in 1825, now with Walter Probert as a tenant It was then sold to Thomas Jones, a carpenter, also of Staunton, for £91.

Thomas Jones held this property when the tithe was assessed, he also owned 4-5 Church Road, The Elms and parts of High Gardens.

In the 1800s the southern part of the house was occupied by tradesmen, butchers and shoemakers, and was probably a shop. By 1871, like the other part of the building to the north, it was rented to agricultural workers. A map of the sewer system of 1900, annotated by William Cartwright, shows the house still divided, with the southern half let to Parton Farm, and the northern to Castle Farm. This was still the case in 1918. R. W. Griffiths, Esq., J.P. , (Castle Farm) rented the southern part and Mr Thomas Hamar (Parton Farm) rented the northern part at an aggregate annual rent of £9. The whole was bought by Mr Tebb for £130. The subsequent ownership is not documented. By the 1930s Charles Carter was living there.

Charles Carter had Oakwood, the whole building. He had a shop in Hay. His son took over from him when he came back from the war.

GLEN PROBERT

I remember Carter living there. There was a daughter, husband, two children, and the grandparents, or grandmother lived there... Mr Carter had a 'shed' shop in the garden...he didn't go out and wire places he just had the shop here and another. His wife used to give piano lessons at 2/6d a time. She tried to teach me, She didn't get very far. I used to hate parting with the 2/6d.

JOAN WILLIAMS

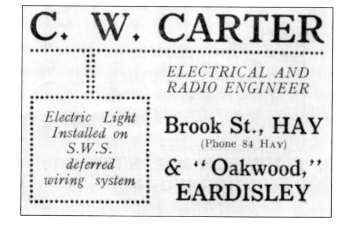

Bridge House

Bridge House is a two-storey, three-bay stone building, probably 18th century in date, laid out on a north–south axis parallel with the road. There is an additional, later, bay, in brick, at the south end and a two-bay, timber-framed cross-wing, covered in rough cast, at the north end.

Three bays of the main range have a roof structure built entirely from re-used smoke-blackened timber, taken, almost certainly, from a medieval cruck hall house probably of 15th century date. The evidence indicates that the hall house was of similar dimensions to the present building, which has the same bay lengths as the earlier house.

The cross-wing was jettied at the first floor on three sides and lavishly decorated on the north and east elevations with curved braces forming a rich pattern of circles. This form of decoration suggests that the cross-wing may date to about 1570-80, which is confirmed by the single tree-ring sample which gave a date range of 1560-1580. It was probably built as replacement solar accommodation for the cruck hall house before the walls of the latter were rebuilt in stone as a two-storey range.

The ownership of this house was in the same family for over 100 years, and is an interesting example of how property passed between generations. As with Oakwood, the boundaries of this property have changed. In the earliest records it consisted of 'the house, a barn, fold and 3 garden panes and an adjoining orchard'.

The first owner in the record is Thomas Godsall, who died in April 1744, but it was not until 1749 that his son William, a butcher, was admitted to the property. William married Mary Heywood in 1746, and had a son, also called William, baptised on 23rd October 1747.

In the February of 1769 William the son married Ann Turner of Eardisley. This was followed later that summer by a rather remarkable sequence of events in which his father died in early June, and it seems likely that his mother inherited the property. Just eight weeks after becoming a widow she was married to the wealthy Phillip Turner of Quistmoor.

Phillip and Mary Turner then went to the Manorial Court in 1771 when they were admitted as the owners. They transferred the house to 'William Godsall, son and heir of Mary by William Godsall, butcher, deceased. With an interest in the property for Mary Turner for her life, then to William and Ann Godsall his wife and William their son'. Mary had moved to Quistmoor and wanted her son to have the house, but she clearly did not want to give it away and miss the opportunity of an income from the property.

William and Ann had another son, Thomas (born 1773), and it was he who inherited the property in 1836, following the deaths of his grandmother, both his parents and his older half-brother. Thomas lived in London when he inherited the house, and he let it to Ann Brown, widowed the year before. She died in 1844. Thomas died in Hereford two years later, but was buried in Eardisley.

It was probably acquired by the Curzon-Herrick estate soon after, and from the 1840s became the home of the village doctor.

Arthur Robert Lomax, head, unmarried, 40, Surgeon <u>*and a good one too.*</u>

Unauthorised entry in the
1861 Census Returns for Eardisley
by the enumerator Phillip Llewellyn

The house was occupied briefly by Henry Brougham Pope, before it was let in 1890 to Quintin Darling at an annual rent of £39 15s.

Dr Quintin Richard Darling, L.R.C.P.I., L.R.C.S.I. & L.M. Irel. moved to Eardisley in May 1889, and served for 44 years as the village doctor. It was said that he attended an average of 40 maternity cases each year, and had seen two generations grow up. Dr Darling was also a skilled woodworker, he made the cover which rests on the font in Eardisley Church.

Madeline Powell and I, we always had to go to Dr Darling when we broke up school and sing Christmas carols. On the windowsill beside the door was two sixpences, an apple each, and Madeline didn't want apples because they'd got an orchard of apples!, and an orange each, but we had to sing two carols at the door.

Dr Darling would grab both of us sometimes, sometimes one of us, I'm sure he had eyes outside the door. There used to be two long hedges, quite big, and we used to try to tuck down and try and get past the gate before he opened the door and grabbed us. He'd say 'Come on. I'm going to give you some lovely sweet stuff', and he'd give us a teaspoon of medicine – goodness knows what it was for – but it was red and sweet, oh gosh! He was a dear old man, he always used to be going mm-mm-mm-mm, and his head would be going.

Lillian Barron

Presentation.- In our last issue, we made reference to the long time, 44 years spent amongst us, and we expressed our good wishes for his years of retirement. Now it is our pleasure to record an appreciation of his long service as a medical man, his social work, and his genial personality. To mark these, a small committee was recently formed. The response was spontaneous and generous, in the villages, there being no less than 100 subscribers. It was a very pleasant evening on Friday, Feb. 1st, when a large company met in the Curzon Herrick Hall. The presentation was made by Mr. Parry in a few well-chosen words, The gifts were made jointly to Dr. and Mrs. Darling, and consisted of a very handsome clock, with a suitable inscription, and also half a dozen dining-room chairs. In a few very touching words, Dr. Darling, accepted the gifts. Other speeches also followed. Thus a long and happy term of office has come to an end.

Weobley and Deanery Parish Magazine
February 1935

Bridge house always used to be one house when the Darlings had it. When Mrs Philpotts retired from the Brook. She was very friendly with Mrs Darling and she wanted to live in the village and they divided the house then. Mrs

Philpotts had her entrance opposite where Bill Kinch lived (Oakwood). Mrs Darling had the side next to the Bridge.

GLEN PROBERT

Dr Darling finished before our time. It was Dr Miller, he built Green Gables in the early 1930s. Dr Darling had his surgery in the bungalow opposite Bridge House,

You belonged to a club, so much a week. We used to go and pay 6d a week to Mrs Povey. I think that was connected with the Doctors.... we joined some scheme, if you had to have an operation and you belonged to this – then you got your operation. If you didn't belong to it I don't know what happened. It was so much a month. When the men stamped their cards they'd [family] automatically come under it, they probably would, it might have been just for the children. When I had my operation, because things all went wrong I was in hospital for some while. I remember Mum talking in the background saying what a good job they were in this.

DORIS WEALE AND DOROTHY JOSEPH

Malt House

The block of land now occupied by the bungalow, The Malt/March House, the village hall, and The Nook or Institute cottage is described in the manorial records as two properties; an orchard and house.

Recently widowed Elizabeth Jones transferred this property to John Jones a carpenter of Staunton on Wye in 1742. He later sold it to the Revd Samuel Bennet and Edward Collins, along with an orchard near the Revd Bennet's house. (See Eardisley House/ White House.)

Revd Bennet gave up his interest in the property two years later, and Collins included his wife Mary. At the time Elizabeth Davies lived in the house, but by 1767, when Edward and Mary mortgaged the property to Thomas Fershell of Tibberton, it was 'in their own occupation'. Later that year their son inherited the property and immediately sold it to Phillip Turner of Quistmoor.

On 26th October 1771 Phillip included this property (and Bridge House) in the entail he created in his will for his new wife and her family.

It was held as one unit by the time of the tithe when it was owned by Ann Lewis.

The property was converted into a garage owned by Richard (Dick) Darling, son of Dr Darling (Bridge House).

Dick Darling and the business he ran have been described by Brian Hales in his book 'Eardisley Characters and Capers'.

The other garage was situated in the middle of the village and was known as "The Modello Garage'. This was owned by Mr. E. Crump and Mr. Gerald Hales who carried out repairs and sold petrol. They also ran the village taxi service and held the contract for transporting the children from outlying districts to school. In 1970 when the business ceased their only employee Mr. E. Williams (Jim) took over the school contract, a job he still continues to do. When the garage was closed down it was taken over by Mr. Hales's son John and partners first of all as car breakers and then Land Rover Sales and spare parts. This was again sold in 1974 to a firm manufacturing aluminium tanks and containers. Mr. Hales now operates his own Plant Hire Service from his premises in the Old Tram Road.

WI SCRAPBOOK 1977

Since then the building has had a variety of uses including being used briefly as a recording studio and later by Roy King for his pipefitting business.

The Eardisley fire brigade was started during the Second World War and the engine was stored in the workshop behind this house before the building of the current fire station in 1966.

The Malt House, with loft entrance, on an undated photograph. The stream is still partially uncovered and in the background the billiard room had not been built. Across the road is the newly rebuilt Central Stores, suggesting a date of between 1903 and 1908.

Malt House – *continued*

The Modello Garage in the 1920s left to right Fred Kite, Gerald Hales, Richard Darling

Darling's garage in about 1939. John Hales, aged about 6, Shirley Hales, aged about 3 or 4, Bob Cowdell, Gerald Hales

The Nook (Institute Cottage)

The relatively small dimensions of the timber used in the construction of this two-bay, two-storey house suggest that it was built in the later 17th or early 18th century. There are chimney stacks at both ends of the range, that to the north including a bread oven. It is possible that the house was built as a pair of one-up, one-down cottages.

This house indicates market encroachment at work as it stands well forward of the earlier building line as marked by the adjacent cruck house, The Forge.

Thomas Harris of Upper House Farm rented this house in 1841, and he also rented other land in the village, in Wooton and in Woodseaves. Most of this was rented from Elizabeth Foley, some from the Revd Coke. He also rented The Malt House and cottage from Anne Lewis, who did not seem to own other property, or live, in the parish. By 1871 a widow, Bridget Beavan, was renting the house.

The President then announced that the House lately occupied by Mrs Bevan had been engaged at a rental of £10 per annum for the purposes of the Institute, and that Mrs Herrick had promised a handsome donation to the funds.

A consideration of a person to take charge of the House was brought under notice of the meeting and it was proposed by Mr R. Edwards, and seconded by J. Jenkins, that Thomas Armstrong, be offered the post of Curator to the Institute, in consideration of having the occupation of the upper rooms of the house and garden, rent free, subject to a month's warning on either side. This resolution was carried.

MINUTES OF GENERAL COUNCIL MEETING OF EARDISLEY CHURCH INSTITUTE. 16TH OF OCTOBER 1877

The Chair then said that the present meeting was called in consequence of an entry in the suggestion book which was handed to him on Saturday night signed by three members stating that there was a report current that the Institute House had been used for gaming and requesting that a council meeting might be called at once to inquire into it. He accordingly issued the notices yesterday for the present meeting and he would ask Mr R. Griffith as one of the members who signed the suggestion book to explain as far as he could the report in question.

Mr R. Griffith then said that Edwards the Police Superintendent in Kington had received a report from Llewellyn at Eardisley that Lewis the Constable had been gambling with Griffin the steward and that Griffin had given Llewellyn the information. Mr Griffith added that Griffin had been questioned on the subject in the presence of several of the members and he utterly denied having given any information of the sort. After some conversation on the subject it was decided that Griffin be sent for to attend the meeting in order that his statement might be heard, and when he came the chairman asked him whether it was the case that he and Lewis had gambled together in the Institute and he distinctly stated he had not. The Chairman then asked whether he had ever played with Lewis and he replied yes in the public room but not in the private room and he had never played for money with him. Griffin then withdrew. The meeting was unanimously of the opinion that the Report was quite unfounded and that there had been no gambling at all on the part of either Lewis or Griffin and further from the observation of those members who are most in the habit of frequenting the Institute no gambling takes place there at all.

SPECIAL COUNCIL MEETING. OCTOBER 27TH 1879

In 1923 an indenture of trust was made between William Curzon Herrick and the Parochial Church Council of Eardisley and signed by the Revd S. Osborn, Dr Q. Darling and Mr A. Vaughan. The document bequeathed land (on which the Curzon Herrick village hall now stands), the coffee tavern and institute 'to provide for the needs and recreation of the poor parishioners belonging the Church of England'.

We moved in forty-eight years ago (1955). It was the caretaker's house for the hall. Mrs Hughes lived there, then Mrs Webb, May Webb. We followed them. Roly Webb, he was a painter and decorator, Mrs Webb was a sister to Miss Parsons who had the laundry across the road.

DOROTHY JOSEPH

Billiard Room and Reading Room

The reading room was built in 1880 and paid for by Mrs Perry-Herrick. The need for this arose from the conversion of the entrance room of the Institute Cottage into a public refreshment room, and the reading room upstairs into a club room.

The building of the billiard room was initiated in 1908 when the chairman read a letter to the committee of the institute from Mrs Herrick stating that she was 'sure that it would be a very good thing to have a larger room at the Institute, and I shall be quite ready to bear the cost when the parish has done what it can'. The plans for the extension of the Institute Room were later submitted by Mr Whitehead for the consideration of the committee.

Details were discussed, the principal being the position of the staircase leading to the proposed room. The decision was that the staircase should lead from the covered passage to the new room. Mr Whitehead assured the committee that the work would be in hand in the course of a few weeks.

There was six or eight of them used to play snooker every night, Jarrett the policeman, and Charlie Nicholas, Bateson the school master, Dummy Jim, and others. The snooker room, was their club, and you could not get in there. Dummy Jim was a carpenter, deaf and dumb, worked for Walter Howells, and lived at Hobby Lyons with his sister.

GLEN PROBERT

Forge

This is one of the largest medieval hall houses in the village. It is a cruck-framed building of three bays laid out on a north-south axis. The south bay, used for many years as a blacksmith's forge, was the service bay (buttery and pantry) with the remaining two bays to the north forming the open hall. A fourth bay, the solar accommodation, originally stood to the north on the site of the present cottages.

This building, with its four pairs of massive cruck blades, is of high quality but with limited decoration. Each bay has long windbraces lapped into the backs of the three tiers of purlins. The central crucks over the hall have an arch-braced collar and chamfered soffits.

The original cross passage survives. There is a large, inserted stone chimney stack which probably stands on the site of the original open hearth.

Tree-ring dating indicates that the building was constructed using timber felled at some time between the years 1437 and 1473.

The front of this building delineates the original edge of the open market area.

This property is not recorded in the manorial record. It was part of the Perry estate in 1841 when it was rented to Thomas Parker, a blacksmith. He was succeeded by his son in the 1850s, and then John Williams and John Element. The next blacksmith was Thomas Burgoyne. An anonymous note found in family papers sketches out his life:

Born 17 April 1884. Apprentice to Blacksmith at Lyonshall, improver at Eaton Bishop. His first job was at Ansells Brewery Aston, Birmingham, later Farrier in mines at Clydach and Llwynpia, Tonypandy. Farrier and Vetinary work at Newham on Severn. He was Blacksmith and Farrier in Eardisley between March 1917 till December 1950.

The Forge in the 1930s

Captain of Kington town football Club 1910 to 1913. Captain Eardisley Football Club 1919 to 1929. Life long Aston Villa Supporter. Die Hard Tory. Great Scrapper. In Fact one hell of a guy.

Thomas Burgoyne bought the forge in the Estate Sale, although there is some doubt of the price he paid:

These books vary – what he paid varies from £210 to £310. I don't know what he really did pay but I know he borrowed money from his brother and not very long after his brother wanted his money back. So he had to borrow elsewhere and in those days people rented. They didn't have what you call 'a monkey on the chimney' which was a loan to buy a house. You just didn't do that in those days.

He was very busy. Very busy. Because he made wrought iron work. There were some gates at Orchard Place, Winforton. He made those. I don't know if they are still there. Very ornamental iron work. He was quite a gifted man and he was very good at shoeing horses, much to the other blacksmith's dismay, because the other blacksmith had all the other work and when Harry's father came he did all he could to stop him.

But he was rude to a farmer and told him to take his horses away and he couldn't do them for a week, but they needed shoeing. So on his way back he called at the new blacksmith and he got a good job done, and told everybody, and very soon the other blacksmith had lost his business. That was why there was the resentment and running up the price of the house. The opposition blacksmith ran the price up of The Forge hoping to get rid of Tom Burgoyne because he lost a lot when he arrived.

Thomas Burgoyne, soon after taking over the Forge, with apprentice Jack Morgan, The Mill

Oh, he was a very keen sportsman, he loved football and was Captain of Kington Town Football Club for a number of years. I still have his watch chain with his medal, and he used to coach school boys in Eardisley in football on Fridays. He was a keen boxer – that was when he was working in Birmingham. He just had a great zest for life.

His son … Doug was caught smoking behind the coal shed at school and he was called into the headmaster who used the cane quite frequently, and he was rude to the headmaster, cheeky, so the head lost his patience and laid on the cane pretty heavily. Bent over, and he just went on and on, until Doug ran out of school down the lane on to the tram line and back up and home. Showed his mother his back which was all red weals and skin broken in several places – and old Betsy had done that – so father got on his bike, leather apron and all, goes off down to the school to see the head about what had been going on and as he walked across the playground the boys were saying 'go on Mr Burgoyne, hit him, Mr Burgoyne!'

The Forge was one of the first houses to have electricity installed. SW & S Electricity were the suppliers. Tom would not have electricity in the bedrooms 'because the children would read' he said. He had it downstairs, so that when we went to bed we had to carry a candle.

He also sold bikes. I remember that Raleigh bikes were £4 something and Hercules were less – a lot cheaper – and BSA were halfway between, and he did cycle repairs and you could buy bike lamps and batteries. He was first to sell petrol in cans before there were pumps. When the garage had the pumps fitted he agreed to give up selling petrol.

JOSEPHINE BURGOYNE.

On the death of Mr. Tom Burgoyne in 1950 his two sons, Harry and Douglas, started to do vehicle repairs as well as blacksmithing at The Forge. They specialised in Diesel engines which at that time were fairly new. Often it was necessary to erect a tarpaulin to keep out the rain as the old Penthouse was too small to accommodate the large vehicles. In 1952 they altered the building to improve working conditions but before long this building proved too small so in 1957 they rented a larger building from Mr. Sharples. As time went on the need for a blacksmith ceased as farm implements became mechanised and horses were almost non-existent in the area.

In 1968 the Burgoyne brothers built a large garage further down the village. The original premises at The Forge were then used as a small showroom and offices.

WI SCRAPBOOK 1965

Old House and Woodbine Cottage

English Heritage date this pair of houses to the 17th century with mid 19th century alterations. The houses are timber-framed with rendered infill of two plus two framed bays. Single storey and attic with dormers. The two houses share a lean-to timber-framed 19th century porch.

In 1918 these cottages were let to William Jenkins and John Thomas at aggregate rents of £11 6s per annum.

The three-house terrace of Woodbine, Old House and forge were occupied by Mr Williams, the two Miss Gwatkins and

Tom Burgoyne. Mr Williams was Col. French's gardener at Winforton. The Miss Gwatkins' father had been foreman blacksmith at the repair sidings at the station. They lived very frugally, taking in washing and selling hen's eggs. Remembering them as archetypal spinsters – 'spinnies', reminds me of one of my many lessons in social history. As a young brash insensitive youth I happened to use a disparaging remark about the old spinnies in the village. My mother quickly cut me down with the sad explanation that many of that generation had lost their sweethearts in the first war. A fact that is easy to confirm by the names on the war memorial.

BRIAN JONES

Granville House and Arboyne House

Arboyne House and Granville House once formed a single unit.

Granville House is a two-bay, two-storey, timber-framed range probably of the late 16th century, laid out on an east-west axis. It also incorporates, on the street frontage, one bay of a three-storey, four-bay range that is aligned parallel with the road.

The east gable of the two-bay range originally overlooked a wide market area but is now hidden following the construction of the main block, a blatant example of market encroachment, suggesting that the building once had a public or semi-public function. This does seem to be the case as the present domestic accommodation has been formed within a building that may have been built primarily as a commercial structure such as a corn store.

The principal part of Arboyne House is formed in three bays of the four-bay, three storey range that is set parallel to the road. It includes a bow-windowed shop front of the 18th century and this may well indicate the date of the rest of the building. The ground-floor walls are of stone but above this there is timber-framing hidden behind rough cast. The surviving evidence, at the centre of the building, of a hoist with trapdoors indicates a past commercial function. The house includes a 17th century staircase and panelling that were added in the 20th century.

Within the wing to the rear of the building there are parts of an earlier timber-framed structure.

Before 1740 the property was owned by Thomas Hall, gentleman. The Halls were an important family in the village, and when Thomas died in 1740 his daughters Elizabeth (married to Henry Wellington) and Ann (married to Henry Colebatch) inherited. Henry and Ann were living in the house at the time, and they were cultivating a two-acre meadow 'now planted with hops', which formed part of the inheritance. This meadow had been known as Taylor's Field, but was later known as Widow's Meadow, and it is this name which is recorded on the tithe maps. The meadow was 'off Phillis Lane which led from Eardisley to Upcott'. Today we know it as the

Eastfield housing development on the Almeley road.

All this property was mortgaged three years later to William Taylor or Tyler of Noke, Pembridge, and when he died in 1748 his 10-year-old son inherited the debt. Henry Colebatch was still cultivating the meadow but the house was now occupied by Phillippa Kent.

Phillippa had an interesting life. She was born into two important local families, the daughter of Humphrey Baskerville of Eardisley and Phillippa Coningsby of Ullingswick, and it was in the latter village that she and her sister Frances grew up. Phillippa returned to Eardisley in 1730, when she married Thomas Kent of Lower Welson. This would have been quite a step down socially. Although Phillippa had property of her own from which she drew an income, Thomas was an illiterate yeoman whose estates were worth no more than £100 per year.

On the 15th July 1736 Thomas was thrown from his horse. He made his will, leaving his estate to his natural son, William from a previous marriage, and died the next morning. The will was contested by a cousin, John Symonds, and litigation followed. Phillippa bore the expense of several court cases, including taking her own attorney, George Coke, to court for overcharging her. Her refusal to pay some of her debts led to her imprisonment for a week in Hereford before her family paid them and she was released. She lost all the court cases and was forced to give up the farm and move to this rented house in the village.

She is buried in the vestry of Eardisley church, her memorial reads:

Phillippa Kent, relict of Thomas Kent, of Welson, daughter of Humphrey Baskerville, of Eardisley Castle, Esq., worn out with male treatment and lingering diseases. She with much charity and Christian fortitude resigned her soul to God, Oct. 15, 1748, aet 63.

The mortgage on the property must have been repaid by Henry and Ann, because in 1754 they were able to sell the house and meadow to John Harris of Eardisley Castle, and his daughter Mary. She married

Edmund Cheese of Lyonshall on May the 24th 1759, and the property was transferred into their ownership in 1780. It is at this point the record refers to the property as 'Shophouse' for the first time. Whether this is simply a change of name, a change from residential to commercial use, or a rebuilding of the property is not known.

When Edmund died in 1803, Mary and her son, Edward, sold the house and meadow to Thomas and Alathea Jeffries of The Grove, Pembridge. They in turn sold it to Thomas Bromage of Eardisley, a linen draper, for £550 in 1810.

In 1828 John and James Powell paid Bromage £900 for the same property. Eleven years later James and Eleanor Powell sold their share to John for £450. John Powell died on the 26th June 1839, intestate and a bachelor. He was buried at Madley, leaving his eldest brother, Richard Powell, a shopkeeper in Kington, as heir. He wasted no time, and was admitted to the property on the 5th July. The tenant at this time were James and Ann Bengree, Grocer and Drapers.

When Richard Powell died in 1848 he left the property to his son James Powell, and he carried on as draper/grocer in the houses until his death in 1866. In his will James left the property to his wife, Caroline, to receive rent for life provided she stay unmarried. This she did, and was able to leave it to her son James Powell, described as a farmer, in 1878. James was to pay the other son John £500 six months after the death of Caroline. He raised this money by mortgaging the property for £500 to Elizabeth Yeoman. Meanwhile John lived in the house and worked as a shopkeeper and maltster. James defaulted on the loan, and on a further loan of £100 from William Humfreys, solicitor, and on 5th October 1886 was adjudged bankrupt. His estate was placed in administration, and Sophia Perry-Herrick paid the debts and received the property.

The shop was rented by John Jay soon after.

In 1918 Arboyne House consisted of the house and 'a capital large modern brick and tiled Bakehouse, fitted with an eight-bushel baking oven, with capital Flour Store over, a large brick-built Store Shed with corrugated iron roof, and Two Piggeries'. It was bought by Benjamin Povey for £300. Granville House was described as the village post office and telegraph office of a 'stone and rough cast Freehold Messuage, containing Lobby Hall with tiled floor, Sitting Room, Postal and Telegraph Office, Sorting Room, Kitchen, Pantry, Larder, Scullery, four Bedrooms and Attic... let to Mrs. Nellie E. Smith, a quarterly Tenant, at £18 per annum' with a proviso that 'the Iron Safe and Post Office Telegraph Fittings belong to the Tenant and are not included in the sale'. This house was also bought by Povey for £320.

May Povey – her father set her up in the sweet shop there and Mr Povey was a butcher over the road and his wife was a very hard working – she used to do a tremendous lot in the shop.

(He owned a number of houses) – and he had some in Hereford as well. But he used to charge them 2s per week for a cottage and when he put it to half a crown – well they thought the end of the world had come, 'he was a miser', he was a this, he was a that!

JOSEPHINE BURGOYNE

May Povey outside the her grocery shop 1926

The top shop (as we used to call it) on the right hand side. The first person that I know of lived there was a man named Jay who also had a son Harley Jay at the other shop down the village.

They lived in the part at the back and over the shop. Povey also had the little shop right down the bottom of the village, next to Burgoyne's garage, and the slaughter house was there, then they came up to the top shop.

May took over the grocery store there. They also had the wooden

Arboyne House in the 1890s. John Jay stands in the door of his general store.

place built, demolished now, where Webb used to be there as shoe repairer. May Povey, well she didn't live there because she wasn't married then. She had the grocery business on her own, her father set her up in that. They had the butcher's shop next to it, the little wooden one. Mr and Mrs Povey lived in Arboyne House.

The shop had bay windows. There were Macintosh's toffee tins and adverts. The bacon was on the right hand side, and the butter, marge – the fats. The side (left) was a fitting with all different things in it, custard powder, cornflower, that was on the upright of the wall. Then you went through the upright of the door, there was a fitting there as well. In the seasons there would be apples in boxes turned on end, and tomatoes – because I have weighed them up many times for May, and all sorts of things, a bit of greengrocery as well. They only sold foodstuffs.

Then the post office moved down to Arboyne House itself. As you go in through the gate there is a jutting piece built out from the main house. That was built for the post office. The post office remained there until it moved down to where Norah had it (Hawthorn), and her mother before her, and her grandmother before that!

LILLIAN BARRON

May married Captain Ellison, the architect, and they continued to occupy the house containing the shop. Mr and Mrs Povey, their son Bruce and other daughter Joan lived in a house which was behind the shop house.

BILL BRIERLEY

Local Honour. - Everyone in Eardisley will join in offering Captain Ellison congratulations upon his deserved honour as the newly-elected President of the Woolhope Club. His keenness and wide knowledge in all that appertains to archaeology, is already well known to very many.

WEOBLEY DEANERY MAGAZINE, VOL 13 NO 2
FEBRUARY 1935

The second grocer's shop is situated at the top end of the village and during the 25 years has changed hands three times but employed in the shop is Mr. Thomas (Nigel to all the locals) who has survived the three owners. Until 1969 the shop was in the hands of Mr. Frank Carter who sold to Mr. Peter Mort. Mr. Mort stayed only three years and in 1972 the business was bought by Mr. Ben Veazey who is still there. Besides Nigel Mr. Veazey, employs two part time assistants. In 1977 this shop was granted an off-licence.

WI SCRAPBOOK 1977

Tram Square Stable and Smithy

This building occupied a prominent position on the Tram Square until its demolition. Historically it was associated with Arboyne House and was included with that property in a transaction of 1878. The Estate Sale Catalogue entry for the Tram Inn lists 'a very substantial and extensive brick, timber-framed and stone-tiled building, now forming stabling for Seven Horses, Forge, Store, Trap House with Three Storage Lofts over, together with a large Cart Shed, built of timber with corrugated iron roof'.

The building formed part of the estate of the Powell family, who owned Arboyne House, when James Powell inherited in 1878. Part of the property was a blacksmith's shop occupied by Thomas Davies. The census records that Davies lived in High Gardens in 1861 and 1817, before moving to the smithy opposite Upper House in 1881.

The Tram Square in the 1900s. The Stable is on the right, with the wooden lean-to shed later occupied by Dick Webb behind the finger post.

Dick Webb's Shop

The shop was attached to Arboyne House, but it's been demolished. I can remember it as Povey's butcher shop and they used to bring the meat up on a trolley. They used to bring it all dressed on this trolley with big wheels and long handles and legs on the handles, they just lifted off the ground and they wheeled the meat up. I often think of all this environmental nonsense! The meat was wrapped in a sheet and cut up at the shop. Mrs Povey was a very good business woman. Mr Povey was a clever fellow, he left the butchering business to his wife.

JOAN WILLIAMS

Dick Webb's shop was joined onto the grocer's shop, Arboyne House. Before Dick Webb came there was a butcher's, and when it was knocked down it still had the original little gate on the door, to stop the dogs going in.

GLEN PROBERT

Dick Webb had all these shoes and never a label on one – he knew everybody's shoes. His shop was a real meeting point; he went on with his work, and people would come in for a chat.

DOROTHY JOSEPH

Adjoining Mr. Veazey's grocery shop is a little wooden building. In this building we have been very fortunate in having for the last 50 years Mr. Dick Webb who has carried on the business of shoe repairing for the village and surrounding area. Not only has he repaired shoes but he has resurrected many pairs of football boots and school satchels. Throughout the years this little shop has been a friendly meeting place for a chat - adults and children alike. It is sad to realize that when Mr. Webb finally retires another of the village characters will be gone never to be replaced.

WI SCRAPBOOK 1965

Turn Pike House

Ye Old Eardisley.

In Eardisley the tollhouse was on the edge of Tram Square and it shows up well in the photograph thought to have been taken in 1867. The gates on the Almeley road and the main highway are behind the tollhouse, and on the right a fence or gate closes the space between the cottage and the stable. Another gatepost with hinge brackets can be seen at the beginning of the Woodseaves road, although this road was not part of the Kington Trust at the time. The building and gates are clearly marked on the tithe map of 1840.

Parliament authorised the setting up of turnpike trusts in the 18th century as a way of improving the road system in Britain. Local groups of landowners, businessmen and gentry who had an interest in improved roads could form themselves into a trust and subscribe their own money to improve the roads. They could erect a gate, or turnpike, across a road and levy a toll on travellers who wished to use a certain stretch of the road. The funds raised were used to pay for further road improvements, and provide a dividend on the investment.

The success of such ventures depended on how much traffic the improved roads would generate, but it was bound to be limited in rural areas where the amount of through traffic was likely to be small anyway. This applied in our area and the Kington Turnpike Trust, founded by Act of Parliament in 1756 had to return to Parliament a number of times to raise more money, principally by raising the charges.

The original tolls on the Kington road were:

Horses, drawing	4d
Oxen, drawing	2d
Drove of oxen	10d per score
Droves of calves or sheep	5d per score
Beasts of burden, not drawing	1d

The Brilley road was charged at half this rate.

By 1773 it was necessary to raise yet more money so the Trustees went back to Parliament for an Amending Act which allowed full tolls to be charged on the Brilley road and established the right to take over the road between Eardisley and Willersley, where another tollhouse was built at what is the T-junction with the Brecon road today. This stone tollhouse later had a brick upper storey added and was in use as a residence until the road junction was widened in the early 60s. It was then in the way and was completely removed.

Local people going about their daily business within the village area or farm workers taking carts of earth, manure or seed to the fields were exempt. Cartloads of lime, however, had to pay the toll. Also exempt were those on their way to church or chapel on Sundays, or going to and from elections.

The coming of the railways, in the 1830s and 40s, saw the beginning of the end of the turnpikes. As their revenues declined the trusts were dissolved, and when the new county councils took over responsibility for main roads in 1888, the upkeep of local roads fell to urban and district councils. (From notes prepared by David Gorvett)

As the census entries for 1851 and 1861 show, it was often the wife, probably assisted by the children, who took on the roll of gatekeeper.

The Kington trust was still in existence in 1876, and the turnpike house had probably been demolished by 1881.

Tram Inn

This is a timber-framed hall house laid out on the edge of the former market area. The hall was very modest in size, with a floor area of about 350 sq. ft. The service accommodation at the southern end has been extended by an additional timber-framed bay whilst the upper end has been rebuilt in brick as a cross-wing. A later floor has been inserted in the hall.

Tree-ring dating has established that the building was constructed using timber felled on or before the winter of 1513. This almost certainly means that it was erected in 1514, a relatively later date for what would have been an outmoded design – most houses by this time had abandoned the open hall with its central hearth.

The deeds of this freehold house have survived, and they reveal a complex history. Ties were made and broken between this house and several other properties, as mortgages and ownership changed hands.

The earliest records show the owner as Thomas Arnold, who settled the property on his second wife, Mary, after his death in 1739. It is not known if his father, also Thomas, had owned the property before him. At the time the house was subject to a complex series of mortgages which included other properties.

The house was purchased in 1750, together with the neighbouring house (Foxpie Cottage), by George Lloyd. It would be another year before he finally settled the outstanding mortgages. George was described as an 'innholder' and had lived in the village for some time. He married Jane in 1739, and was living near Clifton House in 1744.

The tenant at that time was Henry Watkins, a butcher, and the house he occupied is identified by name – Arnold's House.

The vendor was Benjamin Yeates, a wheelwright living in Bristol. He was born in the village in 1720 to Richard and Mary Yeates. Richard was a cooper, and owned other property in the parish. The family also owned the copyhold property next door (now Foxpie Cottage) and at some time Mary Yeates had lived in that house.

So the first evidence of the name of this property, and of its use as an inn, is from 1750. It is also possible to date the change of name to 'The Tram'. The tramroad from Hay to Eardisley did not open until about 1818, and was extended to Kington in 1820. The inn probably changed its name then to cash in on the growing trade to stable and change the horses at halts, and refresh the men.

When George Lloyd died in 1778, he left in his will, 'To my wife, all estate for her life unless she remarries, then all estate equally to four daughters: Mary, Elizabeth, Jane and Ann ... but my opinion for the sake of her children she will I hope in no ways alter her condition'.

The property did pass to the daughters, and Mary's marriage into the large Turner family of Almeley and Quistmoor further complicated the situation. She seems to have retained her share in 1813 when Jane, Elizabeth, and Ann's son George sold their shares of the properties to Thomas Hatton, a butcher. He paid a total of £255 for the ¾ shares. Hatton mortgaged this property to Elizabeth Hughes in 1823. In 1834 Philip Turner sold the last ¼ share to Richard Banks.

Richard Banks is recorded as the owner of the property in the tithe apportionment. He is also listed as the owner of the other properties, Foxpie Cottage (then two cottages), and Clifton House. The latter houses were unoccupied at the time.

In 1847 James Watkins negotiated an absolute purchase of the property for £395 (£295 for the freehold, £100 for the copyhold). The freehold is described as 'the Tram Inn with garden, orchard, and pew'. This is the only example of a private pew in the church linked to a property that has been found in the village. The money for this purchase was provided by a Charles Moro of Kington.

James Watkins seems to have been determined to make a success of the venture. In 1850 he wrote to the Steward of the Perry Estate requesting that the Court Leet for the Manor meet at the Tram Inn. In November of the following year the Court moved across the road from the New Inn. The reaction of the landlord of the New Inn, William Bryan, to this can be imagined.

Despite his attempts to build up the business, when Watkins died on the 18th March 1871 his personal estate could not pay his debts. Some of the debts were paid by a mortgage of £663 10s 4d from William Yeomans of Stretton Sugwas, and over the next few years this mortgage and others were repaid by his widow, Ellen Watkins. Her finances were still in a parlous state and in 1894 she applied successfully to the Foresters Club of Eardisley for a mortgage of £250.

Ellen Watkins died in 1888, and her children inherited. William was a station master in Gloucestershire, John Tudor lived in Wolverhampton and it was left to the daughter, also Ellen, to take over the Tram. She married James Baird on 29th April 1890.

The financial difficulties which had beset the family were finally resolved when Mrs Perry-Herrick agreed to purchase the property for £1800 in 1891. Of this £250 was in discharge of the mortgage to the trustees of Foresters. £380 15s 4d to William Watkins and Edward Morgan as executors of Ellen Watkins. £50 to Bernard Philpin and C H F Christie, trustees, and £1,119 4s 8d to William Watkins, J T Watkins and Ellen Baird.

The two pubs in Eardisley were closed on Sunday because Mrs Herrick did not approve. Workmen used to spend their wages on the pub instead to taking them home. So she closed them on Sundays, and they used to go to Winforton.

JOSEPHINE BURGOYNE

Ellen continued as a tenant, on a rent of £30 per annum, until the estate sale when she was able to buy the Tram Inn including 'detached brewery and Brewhouse, Corn and coal house, garden adjoining building used as stables and forge, store, trap house with storage loft over and cart shed' for £1,250. The village inns were not only places for recreation, they were also the venue for important social functions.

There were a lot of farmers' dinners, and other things going on, and the big room at The Tram was set apart for that sort of thing. They had the Fox Pie dinner there ... well it seemed a lot bigger then than it is now! The bar wasn't in there, the bar was at the back of The Tram; the other room used to be Mrs Baird's private sitting room, where the public bar is now.

JOAN WILLIAMS

They had a pot man and his name was Mr Baynam, and they had a lady living in the house, (this was in the years that I know), Mrs Lawrence, and she had a daughter. She was a divorced lady – which wasn't heard of much in those days. Hilda, the daughter, and I were the same age.

I tell you what was there. Mrs Baird had, you've seen them on antique shows sometimes, those big musical box things. Hilda and I used to go there quite a lot then and it had butterflies on the top, and when it was playing these tunes the butterflies would all be flying, or supposed to be flying. We used to listen to that a lot, we played all old songs on it. It was a grand old thing. I don't know what happened to that, it would be worth some money. I reckon that belonged to the Watkins family, quite a big thing.

LILLIAN BARRON

He would come round to my father, 'Mr Williams, could you spare a penny?' You could give him half a crown, he wouldn't have it, he'd throw it away. All he wanted was a few pennies and he was quite happy. He was a tall, thinnish, man. Children couldn't converse with Fred, as grown-ups could who understood. Fred always went round with his thumbs hooked into the armholes of his waistcoat.

JOAN WILLIAMS

Ellen Baird died on the 22nd March 1939 in the house in which she had been born and where she had lived her life.

Ellen and Frederic Baird at the doorway to the Tram Inn.

Fred Baird, Mrs Lawrence and Hilda Lawrence in the Tram trap

31

I remember mother going to the furniture sale at the Tram Inn, I believe after Mrs Baird had died, where she bought a table for 5/-. When one of the workmen went to collect it with a horse and cart a drawer slipped out of it which contained mainly bone handled cutlery, some of which we still use.

JOHN MORRIS

The Tram Inn is a tied house. In 1952 Mr. Gordon Parker took over as licensee and at that time it was a Trouncer's house. Mr. and Mrs. Parker left in 1961 and Mr. Pete Stockwell took over. He stayed until 1965 when Mr. and Mrs. Parker returned. During this time Trouncer's Brewery were taken over by Ind Coope who in turn were taken over by Ansell's. Like most locals the Tram runs a darts team, has a thrift club and runs sweepstakes for the various big races. The highlight of the Tram's activities are the Harvest Festivals which Mrs. Parker organises and which are held in the lounge. All denominations take part, the service being shared between Father Chadwick, the Catholic priest and Revd Willford. Afterwards the produce is auctioned and the proceeds given to the Church. Mr. and Mrs. Parker have announced that they intend to retire next year and move to their house in Hereford.

WI SCRAPBOOK 1965

Foxpie Cottage

Originally a single-storey, possibly four-bay, cruck hall house, probably built in the early to mid 15th century, Foxpie cottage has had the roof raised and a floor inserted to create first floor accommodation. The original eastern service end has been replaced by a single bay, perhaps of 17th century date, complete with a massive chimney stack and bread oven. There are indications that there was a now-lost solar bay at the west end.

The history of this property mirrors that of the 'Tram'. In 1750 the house was occupied by Mary Yeates. When she died her son Benjamin sold it to George Lloyd for £10. His daughters each inherited a quarter share of the estate in 1813, and with it this house now occupied by William East. The house was empty in 1841, but let soon after to William Meredith. When that estate was consolidated by James Watkins in 1847, he paid £45 for this property. All Watkins property was mortgaged to the Perry-Herrick estate in 1890. In the estate sale the cottages were sold to Robert Haden Tebb of Mayfair, for £135.

The people that lived in the house next to the chapel and the Tram it was Nurse Worthington with the parrot, and the old lady in the next cottage was Mrs Lloyd. I expect Mrs Lloyd was old, I don't know when they dressed like they did. Bonnets and all that. Nurse Worthington was probably in her 40's when she lived there.

LILLIAN BARRON

In 1921 Tebb sold the houses to Sophia Stanford of Wimbledon for £365. The next owner was Hugh Welson of The Beeches, Eardisley, who paid £450 in 1927 for The Nook and The Nest as they were then called, with Miss Thomas as tenant. Miss Thomas still held both the tenancies when Mr Welson died in 1961 and Cartref and Sunfold were sold to Arthur Prosser for £700.

Mr Prosser was the Eardisley roadman who normally was out on the parish roads, but always attended to the village street on Saturday mornings with broom, shovel and wheelbarrow.

BRIAN JONES

The house was still undivided when Watkins took possession, but he must have split it into two soon after. The house remained divided until it was bought in 1983 by Samuel and Avril Morgan (a young married couple, he an architect). They removed staircases from each cottage, altered various walls and doorways (including the entrance to the smaller eastern cottage) to provide a central staircase and central main entrance to what became a single residence. The doorway to the western cottage was blocked up, and fireplaces were opened up to create inglenooks at both ends of the house. A bathroom was installed and the lean-to kitchen was removed

The next owners were the Morgans, who sold it to Dr and Mrs Spencer in 1984. They added a utility room to replace the wooden lean-to shed adjoining the Tram Inn and had the small garden between the house and the chapel (at the west end) excavated to provide an asphalted area as parking for a car and the caravan which they then owned.

Chapel House and The Firs

The record for this property is rather fragmentary, only four transactions have been identified. The identification is by comparison with the tithe, and from 'Bradfield', who owned the property in the 18th century and is identified as a neighbour in the records of the properties to the east and west.

There is no other mention of Bradfield in the Manorial Records, but a John Bradfield is recorded at the Quarter Sessions in Hereford on the 12th December 1737 where he was named in two indictments. The first for 'breaking down of some poles of Thomas Hall', landlord of the Steps Inn. The second crime was much more serious and involved 'assaulting and beating of him the said Samuel Bennet'. It seems Bradfield turned his fury on the Reverend Bennet, the vicar, when he intervened in the original argument.

The owner in 1801 was John Sheldon who died in possession of a 'house, garden and orchard formerly belonging to Bradfield'. The property passed to his widow, Ann, and then their son, Thomas. The property was mortgaged two years later to James Spencer of Hay, and there was a further mortgage of £40 between the same people in 1824.

Ann died in 1837 and her daughter Sarah inherited. Sarah had married a James Fiddy and was living on the Hackney Road in London. She sold the property to James Barrett of Welson, a timber merchant, for £105.

Despite being described as a cottage in 1801, there were three tenants at the time of the sale to Barrett: Richard East, William Jones and David Higgin.

The cottages were sold as part of the Perry-Herrick estate to Mr Triffit for £150, and were described as two small shops let to Charles Haynes and John Saveker, at rents aggregating £13 per annum. George Triffit was married to John Saveker's daughter Marian.

And then there was the Saveker's shoe shop in Chapel House. They owned this house (The Elms) as well, the chapel people.

MARY PRICE

John Saveker was born on September 26th 1837, being one of a family of nine children. His mother was the daughter of the Rev Thomas Rees, pastor and teacher for over 40 years to the Goff's School in Huntington.

Very early in his life he was apprenticed to a saddler and was sent to London as an assistant in an Army Saddlery establishment. He returned to the family home at Eardisley to set up business and there married Elizabeth Underwood of Dilwyn who he had met as a local evangelist. Elizabeth was, for a while in her youth, an elementary school teacher but became an evangelist in the cause of Primitive Methodism. Before her marriage she had travelled the greater part of England and Wales on religious work, but was particularly well-known in the Western counties and South Staffordshire. She had a great reputation as a preacher with a natural talent and ability that carried her congregations along with

her, moving them both to tears and laughter.

After her marriage to John Saveker she devoted her time to her husband and family. John continued the preaching work throughout the locality, walking thousands of miles to preach at small chapels scattered along the Welsh Border. But together their aim was to build a Methodist Community. This they achieved by holding services in the front room of their home, thus the name "Chapel House" was given to it, which it still retains to today. Then along with Mr. & Mrs. John Jay they collected money towards the building of a Chapel.

John Saveker cut the first turf for the foundations of the chapel from the ground which was part of their garden and the four corner stones were laid by: Mr John Edwards of Kington, Mr John Saveker of Eardisley, Mr. John Jay of Hay-on-Wye, Mr. James Morris of Hay-on-Wye. This was in 1866 and the Chapel was opened on August 4th 1876. The first Minister to take up the position was Revd George Middleton.

SCHOOL PROJECT BY REBECCA STEPHENS, DESCENDENT OF JOHN SAVEKER

Mr John Saveker at 94

In those days you could have a good pair of shoes made by Saveker's, and a pair of leggings. Because it was always britches and leggings in them days, walking with the horses, no wellingtons or anything like that. Round about 5/- or 7/6, a pair of good hobnailed boots that would last you a couple of years if you keep plenty of mutton fat on them.

EDGAR LANGFORD

Mrs Elizabeth Saveker

The Savekers had the two daughters, Polly and Patty. Mrs Saveker had the bottom part and I know there was a shed at the back where he worked when he was young man.

They had the window in the room where they sold shoes. You could buy working boots, shoes, slippers. It wasn't very big, believe me, it was crowded. They had shelves of them. They would have a big long strip of wood with hooks on it and there would be men's boots hanging on them, and before wellingtons came in there were just big high boots. Slippers would be hanging on these strips of wood with hooks on them. I used to go there a lot then. I was the only child in those houses at that time.

The next house to the Savekers' was Mr Haynes. He was a shoe repairer, the only shoe repairer (at the time). He had a daughter. She was a Sister of Mercy, in London, and her name was Sister Winifred Haynes. When his wife died he had nobody so she got 'let off' but she always wore her uniform as a Sister of Mercy and she kept house. I used to go down while she took a walk in the evening and stay with the old man.

LILLIAN BARRON

Clifton House

The history of this property is unclear. The Manorial Record lists an Edward Pritchard living in a property in this area in 1730 which was owned by Joan Powell. She gave a share in the property to her son, George Lloyd. When Joan died in 1744 he inherited the property outright. The occupant was a Martha Howles or Howells. It was later occupied by Jane Davies.

The deeds for the Tram Inn mention a release of a freehold and copyhold mortgages in 1814 which notes that 'A cottage has since been erected on part of the ground whereon the said two copyhold cottages stood and do now consist of three dwellings'. This is may indicate the building of Clifton House.

The property became part of the estate divided between George Lloyd's daughters, and the ownership pattern after this mirrors the Tram Inn and Foxpie Cottage. The tenant at the time of the tithe was William Meredith, who also rented Foxpie Cottage.

From about 1895 the house was the police station, and the home of PC William Hadley, PC1, of the Herefordshire Constabulary.

PC William Hadley, PC1, Herefordshire Constabulary, patrols the Tram Square. (Note the doorway to the Tram Inn to the north of its current position).

Cruck House

This two-bay, two-storey, cruck-framed house probably dates to the first half of the 15th century. The service bay at the east end has been lost but the hall and solar bays survive. At the east end, in the corner of the formerly open hall, a large stone chimney stack, possibly of 16th or 17th century date, and bread oven have been inserted along with the first floor. The framing on the front of the building is also later although it may copy elements of the original structure.

The hall of this medieval house is small, some 330 square feet, when compared with The Forge, (570 square feet) and 1–3 Church Road (520 square feet) but large when set against Birdswood at 260 square feet.

Despite its relatively small size this was a property of some distinction, described in the records as a 'mansion house containing the Hall, and the entry or pantry, and the Lower Chamber'. In 1720 it was owned by John Meredith, of Eardisley, a haberdasher, and occupied by his sister Kathleen. John also owned the adjoining garden and the large field to the rear of the house called the Sheepcroft.

It was bought by John Pugh for himself and his daughter Elizabeth but occupied by Richard Edey. Pugh only seems to have acquired a half part of the gardens.

In 1744 the house was made over to Elizabeth and her new husband, Benjamin Prees. They lived in the houses, but must have been in some financial difficulties as they mortgaged it the next year to James Lloyd Harris, a Kington attorney. It was then sold to Barnaby Jones, yeoman, and his wife Joanne, of Almeley in 1757. Barnaby died in 1776 and the property was bought by John Baker.

There is an unfortunate break in the Court Rolls until January 1814 when the property passed to William Downes of Hereford. He died on the 17th January 1814 and the property passed to his daughter, Martha Clee Downes, also of Hereford.

The occupier was William Langford and his wife Ann, and they were still there in 1839 when the tithe apportionment was made. Up to about 1820 William Langford lived in the west part of The Holme, his name was recorded when the property passed from Joseph Price to William Price for £18

There may be a link between the Langfords and the Pugh family who owned the house in the 1700s. In the mid 1770s there are mentions in the record of an 'Ann Langford widow of Richard Langford, daughter and heir of Thomas Pugh', in connection with the sale of The Malt House.

By 1861 Thomas and Jane Postings were the young tenants in their twenties and they remained there until they died in about 1915. Thomas was a sawyer and later became a fruit merchant. The house belonged to the Perry-Herrick estate for most of their tenancy. By 1918 it was let to Mrs Bailey at £5 per annum. It was bought by Mr Tebb for £145.

The next property was known to us as the glasshouse, since in those days it had an enclosed glass vestibule across the front and was the home of a lady who ran a nursery school and, I am led to believe, ran some sort of fostering/adoption scheme. Strangely enough my aunt of latter years probably had the enclosed veranda fitted when she moved to the village from London seeking relief from her arthritic pain. While I was still at school the property changed hands again and Mr Dawkins an accountant came and the glasshouse disappeared.

BRIAN JONES

Rose Cottage and Ivy Cottage

This pair of cottages was built in the 19th century. They were sold in the Estate Sale to William Cartwright for £280. Cartwright had rented Rose Cottage; Reginald Still rented Ivy Cottage, at £7 10s each. Reginald Still worked as a baker in Triffit's Stores (see Central Stores) and married into the Cartwright family.

Mr Cartwright's Record. 90th Birthday Celebration.
On the eve of his 90th birthday Mr W Cartwright, the grand old man of Eardisley, was presented with an armchair by his many friends and members of the parish council in appreciation of a remarkable record of service to the parish.

For 56 years he was clerk to the parish council, and, in addition to being assistant overseer in Eardisley for 34 years, he acted in a similar capacity for a similar period in Willersley, and for eight years in Winforton.

He was registration officer of electors for Eardisley and Willersley for 36 years and for Winforton for 34 years was presiding officer at Parliamentary elections three times, three times poll clerk for Kington Rural District and parish council elections and four times census enumerator for Eardisley, Winforton and Willersley.

But this is by no means all. For 75 years he was a Church bell ringer, for 20 years a manager of the Eardisley Church of England school, 36 years National Health Insurance Secretary, 45 years secretary of the Druids Benefit Society, for a long period he was a member of the Church Choir and his other appointments include the secretaryship of the bellringers fund, the sports club, the quoits club and the football club.

HEREFORD TIMES 1953

Eardisley Quoits Club in 1909. Standing, left to right W. Gummer, W. Philpotts, C. Philpotts. Seated: J. Southgate, W. Cartwright (Secretary), J. Element and son, J. Watkins (Captain)

Northview

This house was a 'messuage of garden, orchard and two Burgages', and on the tithe map the property also included the land on which 'Fairview' bungalow now stands.

In 1733 it had been occupied by Thomas Taylor when the owner Ann Ridgeway, a widow, sold it to Margaret Pugh. She soon sold it to a John Shutor. The tenants at this time were Hottoft and Anne Fenton. In 1757 Shutor died and his son, also John, inherited. He then sold it to Henry Allen, a parson, of Almeley. Reverend Allen sold to Richard Edmonds in 1767, who sold to Richard Coke in the same year. About this time the tenant was a John Jones, a glover, and it was to another glover, William Lloyd, that the property passed in 1772. The house remained in this family for some time, passing, along with other properties in the village (Brook House where William Lloyd senior lived), to the son William and his wife Elizabeth in 1792 with the death of William senior. An entail in his will specified that it should pass to their daughter Elizabeth in turn.

Whether or not it did is not recorded, but William was still in occupation in 1806. By 1826 it had been sold to Samuel Phillips, the tithe described it as 'house, shop, garden and orchard'. Samuel Phillips was a wheelwright and he lived in the house up to the 1860s. The census gives subsequent occupants.

It was bought with other property by Sophia Perry-Herrick from Jane Phillips for £310 in 1886. In the Estate Sale, it was a 'detached Cottage of 8 rooms with lean to washhouse, garden, poultry yard, orchard and timber shed and let to William Tantram at £12 p.a.'. He bought the property for £240.

Freda Watkins, her father was a brother to Mrs Baird, he was the station master in Kent, I think. They bought Northway.

LILLIAN BARRON

Mr Tomlinson lived in the next cottage, which was at right angles to the road, with his wife Edith, who was another daughter of John Saveker. Mr Tomlinson became another electrician and used the room in his cottage next to the road as a shop. Mrs Tomlinson also gave piano lessons and I was a pupil of hers.

BILL BRIERLEY

Electric Light.- The tender of Mr. Tomlinson for this work has been accepted by the Committee, as it was considerably below that of the rest…We understand that there is no probability that the electric power will be available in the village before the end of 1931 at the earliest. To say otherwise is only to create fresh disappointment.

WEOBLEY RURAL DEANERY PARISH MAGAZINE
OCTOBER 1931

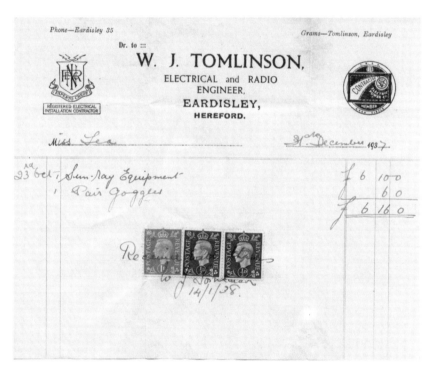

Knapp House (Knapp Cottage)

These cottages are not listed by English Heritage, and their construction date is not known.

The history of this house is well documented in the manorial record, and is the only house in the village which has retained its original name from the 18th century. The property is nearly always described as a "house, garden and fold".

In the early 18th century the house was in the possession of the Protherough family. This family is found in the earliest parish registers, where the deaths of Margaret, Walter, Thomas and Evan are recorded between 1639 and 1647. There is no

indication of if, or how, these people were related, and what relationship they had with the two branches of the family that developed through Thomas and Ales (Alice) and Edward and Rachell from the middle of the century. The family went on to be significant landowners in the parish, with property in Upper Welson, Willersley, The Dukes, as well as other houses within the village.

Although they are not recorded as owners in the manorial record the Knapp House probably belonged to Thomas and Ales, and it was certainly in the possession of their son Thomas (born 1650) by 1710. On the death of his wife Elizabeth in 1714 Thomas gave his son John an interest in the property. In turn, John passed it on to his son Thomas in 1745.

The records hint at a relative decline in the status of the house during this period. What might have been a substantial property in the 17th century, was not of sufficient standing for a respectable family a hundred years later. Thomas did not live in the house as it was described as being 'in the possession of Samuel Lewis in the village'.

Thomas passed the house on to his brother Samuel when he died in 1750. Samuel Protherough continued to rent the property out, but he evidently had financial problems, and the house was mortgaged to Judith Preece of Wellington, Hereford in 1771. The tenants at about this time were Samuel Lewis and later John Jones.

This mortgage had not been discharged when Samuel died in about 1805. The house was sold by his heirs, son James and daughter Elizabeth, and Judith Bird (nee Preece) to James Vaughan and his daughters Margaret and Ann. The house was then occupied by William Langford. By the time James Vaughan died in 1826 the tenant was a John Watkins. The house passed to Vaughan's daughter Ann (and her husband John Wilton) who then sold it to Thomas Meredith, a shoemaker of Dorstone for £114.

This did not prove to be a sound investment as Thomas, now a shoemaker in Glasbury, sold it in 1836 for only £104 to Thomas Phillips of Newchurch who also owned other property in Willersley. The tenant was then John Faulkener; by 1840 the tenant was William Wall. The census goes on to list the subsequent tenants, and that the house was divided into two in the 1860's.

There is a gap in the records until the house is mentioned in the will of John Edwards of Upper House, and left with other property in the village to his son Jeremiah Harris Edwards. The property is described as 'two cottages known as the Knapp House'.

In 1912 James Hughes and Mrs Rogers lived in the houses when they were mortgaged with The Elms and Widow's Meadow to Jane Parry and John Morgan of Hay for £1300. Jeremiah died in 1922 and the cottages passed to his wife Jessie and his son Basil. In 1924 they sold the house to Samuel Preece of Upper House. The tenant was then John Charles Jones.

Canon Ford Avenue

The year 1952 saw the completion of a council housing estate of twenty-two houses to be known as Canon Ford Avenue. These were the first local authority dwellings in the parish and were all three bedroomed family type houses. This estate was built in two separate schemes by two different builders, the first scheme using a newly constructed well for its water supply. This, however, proved insufficient when the second scheme was completed and the services of a water diviner were sought. These were forthcoming in the person of Alderman William Davies of Castle Farm who located a source in the back garden of what is now No. 11 Canon Ford Avenue. This was subsequently confirmed by Mr. George, a water engineer of Kinsham Presteigne, who later sunk a borehole from which has been obtained a continuous supply of pure wholesome water.

WI SCRAPBOOK 1977

Green Gables

Green Gables was designed by Bettington and Son, architects, of Castle Street, Hereford, in 1936 for Dr Miller.

Dr Miller had a surgery attached to the house at Green Gables, you went in through the side of it. I suppose for those days it was very, very modern. It had a dispensary room, a room where he kept all the medicines, and a waiting room.

DOROTHY JOSEPH

When Dr Darling retired Dr Miller came and built a new house and surgery known as Green Gables. He was an ex-military man and I remember him coming to see Doug James, a boy I went to school with. He had appendicitis diagnosed by Dr Miller and he loaded him up in his car and delivered him to Hereford Hospital to have the operation. And you talk about the National Health Service!

When Dr Miller retired as a practitioner, Dr Smith took over and as a youth I used to suffer with boils on the back of my neck. Dr Miller used to treat them, and he would squeeze them, and it wasn't funny! Dr Smith took a blood sample off me and sent it away for analysis. It came back, he gave me an injection and I never had another boil. Which was a sweet relief!

DENIS LAYTON

High Gardens   6   5   4 Foresters Cottage 3   2   1

		6 High Gardens	5 High Gardens	Foresters Cottage	3 High Gardens
1841 CENSUS		James Evans, 85, Agricultural Labourer. Mary Evans, 35.	William Pugh, 60, Stonemason. John Pugh, 30, Agricultural Labourer. Mary Pugh, 35. Jane Pugh, 8; John, Pugh, 2; Anne Pugh, 4m.	Thomas Herrick, 30, Pot seller. Anne Herrick, 25. Caroline Herrick, 8; Thomas Herrick, 6; Jarvis Herrick, 4; Joseph Herrick, 2; Hugh Herrick, 2m.	Joseph Wall, 60, Agricultural Labourer. Sarah Wall, 40. John Wall, 11; Sarah Wall, 6; Joseph Wall, 9; Emma Wall, 7. John Wall, 40, Agricultural Labourer. Anne Jenkins, 80, Inmate Pauper.
①		Richard Powell.	Richard Powell.	Richard Powell.	Richard Powell.
②		James Evans.	John Pugh.	James Evans.	James Wall.
1851 CENSUS		Mary Evans, 52, Seamstress. James Bowyer, 30, Journeyman Shoemaker. Sarah Bowyer, 25, Milliner.	Thomas Herrits, 40, Earthenware dealer. Caroline Herrits, 17, Housekeeper. Thomas Herrits, 15; Joseph, Herrits, 12, Assistants to their father. Hugh Herrits, 10; Eliza Herrits, 8; Mary Ann Herrits, 4, Scholars. William Herrits, 2.	Walter Watkins, 41, Journeyman Shoemaker. Jemima Watkins, 38. John Watkins, 7, Scholar. Ann Watkins, 3; Charles Watkins, 12m. William Pugh, father in law, 73, Pauper on parish relief.	Robert Wall, 26, Agricultural labourer. Sarah Wall, sister, 24, Milliner. Joseph Wall, 53, Agricultural labourer. Sarah Wall, 50, Laundress. John Wall, 21, Idiot. Sarah Wall, 14, Scholar. John Wall, brother, 55, Agricultural labourer.
1861 CENSUS		John Jones, 44, Shoemaker. Elizabeth Jones, 38. William Jones, 15, Agricultural labourer and farm house boy. John Jones, 12, Farm house boy. Elizabeth Jones, 5, Scholar.	James Pugh, widower, 57, stone mason. Hannah Pugh, widow, 66.	Thomas Davies, 44, Blacksmith. Jane Davies, 44. Thomas Davies, 18, Blacksmith. Ann Davies, 8; Elizabeth Davies, 7, Scholars. William Pugh, widower, 17, Mason. Hugh Herriots, widower, 19, Labourer.	John Kedward, 34, Carpenter. Mary Ann Kedward, 30. John Kedward, 9; Mary Ann Kedward, 6, Scholar Jane Elizabeth, Kedward, 2. John King, widower, 26, Sawyer. John Chance, widower, 36, Carpenter.
1871 CENSUS		Mary Kedward, 38, Carpenters wife. John Kedward, 19, Carpenter. Jane Kedward, 12; Lucy Kedward, 9, Scholars. Thomas Griffiths, lodger, 23, Drainer.	Henry Marshall, 28, Agricultural labourer. Eliza Marshall, 24, labourer's wife. Emily Marshall, 3; Charles Marshall, 1.	Thomas Davies, 54, Blacksmith. Jane Davies, 53. Charles Watkins, 17, Blacksmith. James Saunders, 57, Agricultural labourer. Mary Saunders, 56, labourer's wife. Thomas Saunders, 31, Family servant.	John Owens, 37, Labourer. Eliza Owens, 33. Emily Owens, 7. John Higgins, 68, Shoemaker.
1881 CENSUS		Samuel Davies, 37, Railway Repairer. Martha Davies, 38. Elizabeth M. Davies, 12; Thomas Davies, 10; Ann Davies, 7, Scholars. Sarah J. Davies, 2.	Henry Marshall, 37, Railway Repairer. Elizth. Marshall, 33. Charles Marshall, 11; Henry Marshall, 9; Edwin Marshall, 7, Scholars. Thomas Marshall, 5; William Marshall, 2; Ellen Marshall, 1.	Thomas Griffiths, 44, Maltster. Ann Griffiths, 46. James Griffiths, 14. John Griffiths, 8, Scholar.	John Owens, 46, Roadman. Eliza Owens, 43. Elizabeth Jones, Boarder, widow, 36, Seamstress.
1891 CENSUS		Samuel Davies, Widow, 49, Railway platelayer. Elizabeth Davies, 22. Sarah Davies, 12, Scholar.	Henry Marshall, 50, Railway platelayer. Elizabeth Marshall, 45. Edwin Marshall, 17, Railway platelayer. William Marshall, 12; Ellen Marshall, 10; James Marshall, 5; Leonard Marshall, 6; Elizabeth Marshall, 4. George Marshall, 3.	Harriet Harris, Widow, 90, Living on own means. Henry Harris, 35, Labourer.	Elizabeth Walters, Widow, 77, Living on own means. Sarah Chance, Widow, 45, Living on own means. Ada Chance, 12; Amos E Chance, 9, Scholars.
1901 CENSUS		Samuel Davies, 58, Railway labourer.	Henry Marshall, 56, Railway platelayer. Elizabeth Marshall, 52. James Marshall, 18, General labourer. Leonard Marshall, 16, Grocers Assistant. Elizabeth Marshall, 14. Henry Marshall, Grand Son, 9. Lillian M. Marshall, Granddaughter, 4.	Unoccupied	Mary Dale, widow, 72. William Davies, boarder, 16, errand boy.
③					Edward Higgins.
④				Mr. Wakefield	

① TITHE OWNER   ② TITHE TENANT   ③ 1918 SALE   ④ PURCHASER

Old Forge **The Elms**

2 High Gardens	1 High Gardens	Old Forge	The Elms
Unoccupied	Charlotte Price, 50, Laundress. Jane Price, 15. Mary Price, 9; William Price, 1.	Richard Duggan, 35, Agricultural Labourer. Anne Duggan, 40. Mary Lloyd, 80, Inmate Pauper. Richard Owens, 60, Tinman. Jane Owens, 45. Sarah Owens, 13; Richard Owens, 8.	No record found
Thomas Jones.	Richard Powell.	Richard Powell.	Thomas Jones.
Omwell Lloyd.	Charlotte Price.	John Sarah?	John Sarah?
William Wakefield, 42, Cooper. Susanna Wakefield, 28. Thomas Wakefield, 6; William Wakefield, 5, Scholars. Mary Wakefield, 3; George Wakefield, 9m.	Joseph Price, 22, Brickmaker journeyman. Ann Morris, 23, Laundress. John Morris, servant's son, 5.	Michael Duggan, 78, Pauper on parish relief. Susanna Duggan, 76, Pauper on parish relief.	Thomas Watkins, 45, Saddler. Sarah Watkins, 41. Diana Watkins, 12; Thomas Watkins, 11; James Watkins, 9; Sarah Watkins, 6, Scholars. Caroline Watkins, 2.
William Wakefield, 53, Cooper. Susannah Wakefield, 39. Thomas Wakefield, 16, Cooper. Mary Wakefield, 13; George Wakefield, 10; Edward Wakefield, 8; Maria Wakefield, 7, Scholars. Elizabeth Wakefield, 4; Emily Wakefield, 1.	Elizabeth Price, widower, 40. Elizabeth Price, 19; Mary Ann Price, 15 Epriaham Price, 11; James Price, son, 8; Alice Price, 6, Scholars. Joseph Wall, 64, Labourer. Sarah Wall, 62, Laundress. Emma Wall, 26. Joseph Wall, 28; John Wall, 67, Labourers.	Elizabeth Wall, widow, 66. Robert Wall, 35, Haulier. Richard Wall, widower, 30, Haulier. Diana Wall, 26, Dressmaker. Mary Wall, grand daughter, 4.	Charles Turner, 41, Agricultural labourer. Carolina Turner, 27. John Turner, 2; William Turner, 5m. Joseph Watkins, father in law, 53, Labourer.
Thomas Wakefield, 26, Cooper. Edward Wakefield, 18, Domestic servant.	Richard Price, 28, Labourer. Emma Price, 34. Albert Price, 10m. Joseph Wall, Brother in law, 37. Anne Bache, lodger, 63, Seamstress.	Alfred Davies, 27, Machinist. Jane Davies, 26, Machinists' wife. Alfred Richard Davies, 3; William Davies, 1. Sarah Saunders, 13, General Servant.	Charles Turner, 39, Farm labourer. Caroline Turner, 37. John Turner, 13; William Turner, 12; Elizabeth Turner, 7; Sarah Turner, 4, Scholar. Hannah Jones, niece, 5, Scholar.
William T. Parsons, 29, Sawyer. Sarah Ann Parsons, 30. Elizth. Parsons, 10; Harriet Parsons, 6, Scholars. Charles Parsons, 4; Alice Parsons, 2; Albert Parsons, Son, 3m. John Davies, Brother In Law, 19, Labourer.	Richard Price, 39, Railway Labourer. Emma Price, 44. Albert Richard Price, 10; Jessie Price, 9, Scholars. Joseph Wall, Brother In Law, 47, Raily Labourer Alice Watkins, Lodger, 33, Dressmaker.	Thomas Davies, 37, Blacksmith. Mary Ann Davies, 34. Annie Davies, 10; Alice Davies, 6, Scholars. Thomas Davies, 4; Mary Ann Davies, 3. Jane Davies, Mother, widow, 64. George Jones, 15, Blacksmith.	Emma Shayler, widow, 63. Sarah Shayler, 30, Dressmaker. William Shayler, 23, Plumber & Glazier.
Jane Morris, Head, Widow, 67, Domestic Out servant.	Richard Price, 48, Railway Platelayer. Emma Price, 54. Jessie Price, 19.	Thomas Davies, 48, Blacksmith. Mary Ann Davies, 45. Thomas Davies, 14. Mary Ann Davies, 13; Eleanor Davies, 9, Scholars. Stephen J Lampard, 22, Blacksmiths Assistant.	William Tantram, 58, Railway Inspector. Jane Tantram, 58. Frederick Tantram, 14, Butchers Assistant. Edith Tantram, 9, scholar. Mansell Russell, Grandson, 3. Alfred Nicholas, Nephew, 27, Railway labourer.
Eliza Price, 70.	Richard Price, 57, Railway Platelayer. Emma Price, 60. Jessie Price, 29.	Thomas Davies, widower, 57 Blacksmith. Thomas Davies, 24 Blacksmith. Mary A Davies, 23; Eleanor Davies, 19. George Evans, Servant, 20 Blacksmith worker.	No record found
James Marshall.	Jessie Price.	Thomas Davies	
Mr. Wakefield	Mr. Wakefield	Mr. Davies	

① **TITHE OWNER** ② **TITHE TENANT** ③ **1918 SALE** ④ **PURCHASER**

High Gardens and Foresters Cottage

English Heritage describes numbers 1 (April Cottage), 2 and 3 High Gardens as a row of three timber-framed houses refaced with painted rubble built in the 17th century, and altered in the mid 19th and late 20th centuries. The five bays include a chimney bay (second from the east end) probably forming a lobby entrance to number 1.

Numbers 4 (Foresters Cottage), 5 and 6 form another row of three houses of similar date. These houses have four framed bays of timber-framed walls with painted brick and rendered infill. There is an external roughcast chimney at the west end. Single storey and attic with dormers.

It is a widely held view that these houses formed a 'longhouse' before being divided up. Although these cottages were linked in some way, they probably were not of the classic longhouse type. They will require further study to decode their secrets. The first cottage has what appears to be an original oak staircase, the next has a fireplace with a cobbled base and supporting stones forming the fireplace's outer edge. The cavity has sloping sides, from 7 ft. 6 in. at the front to 5 ft. at the back.

The ownership of these cottages is not well documented. At the tithe apportionment numbers 4 to 6 were owned by Thomas Jones. These became part of the Perry estate and in 1918 they were let to Edward Higgins, James Marshall and Jesse Price on rents aggregating £13 15s. per annum. They were bought by Mr Wakefield for £130.

The rest of the houses were owned by Richard Powell in 1840. They did not become part of the estate.

Historically, these houses were let to farm workers, and later railway workers. They formed a small community of stable families, but there was also a high turnover of occupants in some of the houses. The less than honest sometimes took advantage of this:

The farm workers used to move on regularly. My father was caught out quite a few times. They'd pay for the first few hundredweight of coal and when they were coming to the end of their time, they'd say 'we'll pay you next time'. Many a time he got on his bike and shot off to Nash House or High Gardens to catch people.

DOROTHY JOSEPH

The Foresters Cottage takes its name from the friendly society founded in Eardisley in 1870 under the local branch name of Court Integrity.

By 1901 it had 160 members and funds in excess of £50,000 at today's values. Its annual Fete was always held in June and began with the initiation of new members at the Tram Inn. On this occasion, 3rd June, the initiation was followed at 10.15am by a procession, led by the Band of Hereford Working Boys' Home, to the Parish Church. Canon Palmer addressed them and then they assembled outside for Mr E Hemmings, the Hereford photographer, to take a picture. This done the whole procession paraded the banner of the Society to Parton, Lady Arbour, the Vicarage, Eardisley Park, the Castle and Dr Darling's house ending up at the Tram for lunch. The hosts, Mr and Mrs Baird, served lunch to 110 members in a specially erected marquee. At the entrance to the tent was an archway decorated with May blossom, lilac and laburnum blooms and a large sign proclaiming "Success to the Foresters". At the lengthy celebrations after lunch the only sour note was when a member made some sharpish comment about the inadequacy of the Society's sick pay of 10/- (50p) a week to a labourer with a family to support. The weather for the procession and for most of June was dry and warm which did not make for the best of hay crops. There was none of that "knee-deep in June" look about the pastures in 1901.

DAVID GORVETT 'DAWN OF DAY EARDISLEY IN 1901'

The Foresters' parade outside the New Inn – in 1901.

The Old Forge

English Heritage describe this building as having four timber-framed bays aligned north/south with painted brick infill panels and partly roughcast and weatherboarded. There is a chimney at the junction with the two narrower north bays and the date is probably late 16th century, altered in the mid 19th and mid 20th centuries

The ownership of this house is also unclear: it may be related to the ownership of the plot on which the later house, The Elms, sits to the north. The building seems to have been domestic in the first half of the 18th century, only becoming a blacksmith's in the 1870s. In 1908 Thomas Davies renewed his agreement with the Perry-Herrick estate to rent the blacksmith's shop for £20 annually, but by the time of the estate sale he was only paying £13 10s. He bought it for £120.

We moved there in 1919 I think, just after the First World War. My father didn't buy the forge in the sale; he bought it from someone by the name of Davies, who was the blacksmith then. Davies bought it from the Curzon-Herricks; many people renting their houses were able to buy them then. Davies wanted to retire, my father bought it and he was there until he died.

He was a Master Blacksmith, he learnt his trade with a Mr Brace somewhere near Leominster. He was living at Puddleston before we were born, and he did a seven-year apprenticeship. He got married there and we came along and for some reason he went to the Leysters. But Puddleston and Leysters weren't such big hunting areas as Eardisley, and Whitney and Winforton, and when the forge came on the market he bought it for £600. He had about £400 and he had about £200 mortgage. It was a lot of money because the Parsonage only sold for £675 to Muriel Parry's parents. Yes, and the forge at Kinnersley was sold at the same time and that was £403.

He did shoeing, but he was very keen on wrought iron work, he made the stands for the pub signs. He and Walter Howells, who was the carpenter, they made two beautiful wrought iron chandeliers for the church. Of course my father shod mainly for the hunting fraternity. There were point to point races, that's all gone by the board. Captain Hope at Whitney Court, they were members of the Coates Cotton people; his father left him a lot of money. All his horses came from Whitney to the forge; they kept two grooms at that time. He started his own private pack of hounds, and the hunting fraternity grew and grew around here, the meets on the Tram Square were something to behold.

Captain Hope asked my father if he would consider opening a shop at Whitney, there was a forge at the Stowe Inn, it's a private house today, so that his valuable bloodstock wouldn't have to walk three or four miles to be shod. So my father set up that shop as well. He used to go to Whitney Monday, Wednesday and Friday with his apprentice, and Eardisley Tuesday, Thursday and Saturday morning. Sometimes my father would visit the place to shoe. He used to hire a car from Mr and Mrs Charlie Morris to begin with and then Oliver Jones took over. Bishops at Clifford had a little forge, and he used to go to Sandfords in Winforton.

The Burgoynes were going in my father's time, but Mr Burgoyne specialised in cycles and he had a cycle shop there, tubes and tyres and lamps and pumps.

My father had a very beautiful voice; he was trained and he went to Tenbury College. He sang in the choir here for about 20 years, and whenever there was an entertainment it was always 'Mr Williams is going to sing' and a quiet would come over it. I do remember when I was about 9 or 10 that we had a choir master here, he was also the schoolmaster. He came from Norfolk or somewhere, his name was Mr Collins.

He went to church one Sunday night, and he came home and had a massive stroke, and the doctor then an Irish chap, Dr Miller, said 'He won't last very long', and he was dead by 5 o'clock in the morning. He was 55. That ended it all of course.

JOAN WILLIAMS

The Forge in 1910. The blacksmith then was Thomas Davies.

41

The Elms

In the Manorial Records this property is described as a 'mansion with garden'. In later entries it is named as 'The Elms', but the descriptions may have included an earlier building on the site or neighbouring houses such as The Old Forge.

John Probert lived in the house in 1737 when John Ralphe sold it to Richard and Mary Yeates of Eardisley. They sold it to John and Alice Protherough in 1744, as part of a larger transaction which also involved part of The Dukes and an acre of land beyond Widow's Meadow off the Almeley Road. (See Arboyne House.) John Protherough lived in the property. After his death his grandson John Knowles inherited, selling to William Wilson, an Innholder, the following year. The property was then rented to Esther Austin.

James Evans was living there in 1780 when it was sold to Richard Francis, of Bishops Frome, and his wife Mary. In 1792 they sold to John Baynham, a tailor from Hay; in 1811 it was sold to Robert Phillips of Hereford for £40. By now Hugh Jenkins was living there.

Robert Phillips died in 1825 and Robert Knott inherited. The house was now occupied by Richard Duggan.

Presumably the house was then sold to Thomas Jones, who owned it at the time of the tithe, although there is no entry of this in the record,. The tenant at the time of the tithe was Richard Duggan, and he is also recorded in the 1841 census.

The house passed to John Edwards of Upper House in 1871, and was part of the property disposed of in his will in 1902. His son Jeremiah inherited and let it for a while, before mortgaging it, together with Knapp House and Widow's Meadow, to Jane Parry and John Morgan of Hay for £1,300 in 1912. Jeremiah died in 1922 and the cottages passed to his wife Jessie and son Basil. In 1924 they sold the house to Parry and Morgan for £1000, the remaining sum due on the mortgage.

This house was a post office and draper's, so I've been told; it would be about 1910. Mr and Mrs Billy Nicholas were married and lived here, two lots of them, Bob and Cathy as well. When people got married they often went in rooms with their parents, one up and down. How did they manage? This house hasn't altered much has it, on the outside.

When we bought this there was no toilet, no water. Very few people had water indoors. There was electricity here then, electricity came here fairly soon before the war.

DORIS WEALE

Up the Kington road where a Mr Magnus was living, that used to be the post office. That too had a man named Powell living there and he went up to Hay as postmaster.

I was told that that house was built by someone who lived in the Upper House before I can remember. They had a son who was not quite as he should have been. They had the house built and they had a housekeeper there for him. He was a young man I suppose and the garden wall at the back is built quite high so that he could not get out.

LILLIAN BARRON

Our newspapers used to be delivered all round, a lady on a bicycle from the village, she had them delivered to the house, and then used to cycle out. Her name was Mrs Davies, she lived just up the Kington Road, The Elms. Mrs Davies used to deliver in all weathers, on her pushbike.

MURIEL FENTON

Mrs. Triffit was the last member of the Savager [sic] family, being the youngest of six daughters. On her death in 1962 she added strength to the financial resources of the Chapel by leaving the house in Eardisley known as "The Elms". This house was sold and the proceeds were invested - the Chapel having the interest of the money.

WI SCRAPBOOK 1965

The Elms in 1910. The post office was in the room on the left, a draper's on the right.

Upper House

The house is listed English Heritage as a timber-framed farmhouse. The original part has close-set studding framing, elsewhere the walls have four or five rows of square or rectangular panels. The panels have rendered and painted brick infill. The roof is stone-tiled, laid in diminishing courses. The original central range has three framed bays aligned north/south consisting of a hall with a screens passage at the south end and a solar at the-north end. It probably has 15th century origins.

In about 1600 a chimney was added on the west side, with two diagonal brick shafts, and an upper floor was inserted. A three-bay parallel west range was also added, together with a three-bay south cross-wing with an external rubble chimney on its south side. This wing may have replaced an earlier service wing. A wing of two and a half bays was also added on the north-east. The west range has a jettied first floor on the north end and west side, this side has pendant ball finials and two intermediate posts. The first floor of the south wing is also jettied on shaped brackets at the west end.

For much of the 18th century the farm was owned by one family and tenanted by another.

The owners were the Whitmore family of Haywood. Before 1733 it was held by Thomas Whitmore, and on his death it passed to John Whitmore. In turn his son inherited from him in 1787. The tenants were the Harris family, first Walter, then Susan, and finally by Thomas.

John Whitmore sold it to John Keysall of Temple Bar and Morton Court. He held it until 1801 when it was sold to The Hon Andrew Foley of Hazely Court, Oxford and Newport, and it became part of a large estate that included lands throughout Almeley parish and extended along the road to Eardisley and north to Bollingham.

The Foley family had bought the Newport (or Nieuport) estate in Almeley from the Pember family in 1712. Newly enriched and ennobled, the iron – founding first Lord Foley of Great Witley soon transferred the property to his cousin, Paul Foley of Stoke Edith.

The Hon Andrew Foley, who bought Upper House in 1801, was Lord Foley's third son. He died intestate in 1818 owning the farms at Bollinghill (Bollingham) and Upper House; the latter was let to Mrs Susan Harris Andrew's eldest son, Thomas, inherited and was succeeded in 1822 by William Andrew. In 1828 the estate passed to their unmarried sisters Grace and Elizabeth. At the tithe assessment Elizabeth Foley was the biggest landowner in Almeley with 480 acres, and in Eardisley she owned 1,042 acres. Thomas Harris was followed as tenant in the 1840's by John Edwards. In 1850 the estate passed to Richard Francis Onslow, the archdeacon of Worcester, (who married Andrew Foley's daughter, Henrietta Maria, in 1801) and was sold to the trustees of James Watt Gibson Watt in 1863. The property was mortgaged to Elizabeth Wilkinson, Gilbert Hamlin (or Hamil) and James Muirhead in July 1864.

Upper House was sold when the Newport estate was broken up in September 1909. The farm was let at that time to Mr J C Jones at an annual rent of £338 10s. It was sold again in 1921.

Farmer Edwards of Upper House Farm owned 360 acres and it was his habit to go out regularly to look over his land. He would ride in his pony and cart to make the going easier, and he always took his wife with him. This was not, however, for companionship or advice but entirely for his own convenience. She, poor woman, never rode further than the first gateway. There she was expected to get down and open the gate, shutting it after the trap had gone through. By the time she had done this Farmer Edwards would be well on his way to the next gateway, and so on right round the farm. It is said that one could tell when he was doing his farm round by hearing his loud voice shouting, "Come 'oop, woman" as he urged on his breathless wife to the next field.

TOLD BY GRANDMA PRICE AND MARY PRICE
TO DAVID GORVETT

I can't remember if my father bought it when the Newport estate was sold. Upper House was never part of the Curzon-Herrick Estate. My mother lived at Wooton, she was born a Wooton, and so was I. They went from Wooton to Staunton on Wye, to Lower House; they weren't there long, more than a couple of years, before they came up to Upper House. But mum couldn't stand the place Sometime later we bought Lemore House and the Longdens bought it. Eventually, he was Master of the Hunt.

Most of the people in the village seemed to find jobs in the village, the farmers all had workmen, At Upper House there was somebody in the two Knapp cottages, and two in High Gardens, two over here, three, in the house. He would have had about five or six men, or more. And not very highly paid either mind! Wages were low.

MARY PRICE

Upper House of which a book could be written, but sufficient to say it was a hive of activity with about six permanent staff. There was always something going on and attracted children like a magnet, tractor rides and horses turning out, harvest thrashing, hay treading, rat and rabbit killing. How did we survive?

BRIAN JONES

Upper House in 1907

	Upper House	**New Inn**	**The Holme**
1841 CENSUS	Thomas, Harris, 45, Farmer. John Harris, 45, Independent. Anne Harris, 40. Servants; Charles Knight, 20; John Jenkins, 15; Sarah Green, 15.	John Baker, 40, Butcher. Elizabeth Baker, 30. John Baker, 4. Joseph Baker, 3. William Baker, 1y 3m.	Helen Ball, 20, Dressmaker. Jane Ball, 20, Dressmaker. Louisa Ball, 13, Dressmaker.
①	Elizabeth Foley.	Revd George Coke.	John Powles
②	Thomas Harris.	John Barker.	Philip Llewellyn
1851 CENSUS	John Edwards, 40, Farmer. Ann Edwards, sister, 32, Housekeeper. Susan Smith, 26, General servant. Richard Lewis, 23; Joseph Urall, 18; John Phillips, 16, Farm labourers. James Wall, 14, Waggoner's boy.	William Bryan, 46, Innkeeper, farmer. Mary Bryan, 50, Farmer's wife. Fanny Bryan, 19, Farmer's daughter. Charles Brunt, father in law, 82, Invalid farm labourer. John Powell, 50, Agricultural labourer. Charles Dale, 14, Stable boy.	Phillip Llewellyn, 54, General shop keeper. Elizabeth Llewellyn, 50. Eliza Llewellyn, 26, Shop waiter. Arthur Llewellyn, 14, Draper's apprentice.
1861 CENSUS	John Edwards, 50, Farmer. Jane Edwards, 37, Farmer's wife. Jane Edwards, 6; Jeremiah H Edwards, 4; Ann E Edwards, 3. Samuel Davies, 16, Carter. Alfred Preece, 13, Groom. Eliza Lewis, 18, House maid.	Mary A Whitehouse, 32, Innkeeper. Mary J Whitehouse, 10; Thomas J Whitehouse, 7; Richard T Whitehouse, 4, Scholars. Aaron Whitehouse, 1; Julia A Whitehouse, 1. Honor Davies, 17, House servant. Elizabeth Edwards, 17, Nurse. Edward Beavan, 31, Carter.	Philip Llewellyn, 29, General shopkeeper. Elizabeth Llewellyn, 30, Shopkeeper's wife. Elizabeth Llewellyn, 7m. John, Owen, 28, General servant. Elizabeth Tudor, 17, House maid.
1871 CENSUS	John Edwards, 60, Farmer. Jane Edwards, 47, Farmers wife. Jane Edwards, 16; Jeremiah H Edwards, 14; Annie Elizabeth, Edwards, 13; John James, Edwards, 9. Charlotte Edwards, 18, General Servant.	Thomas Whitehouse, 50, Farmer and Inn Keeper. Mary Ann Whitehouse, 45. Thomas John Whitehouse, 17. Richard Whitehouse, 14. Aron Whitehouse, 11; Julia Whitehouse, 11; William Whitehouse, 8; Louisa Whitehouse, 6, Scholars. Herbert Whitehouse, 2 Eliza Lewis, 24, Domestic servant Lodgers: James Pugh, 67, Stone mason, Thomas Jenkins, 57, Labourer.	Philip Llewellyn, 39, Grocer. Elizabeth Llewellyn, 40. Elizabeth Llewellyn, 10; Mary Ann Llewellyn, 8; Clara Llewellyn 6; Alice Llewellyn, 4, Scholars. Edmund Sheers, Brother in law, 30, Assistant. Thomas Parry, 35, General Servant. ? Preece Servant, 25, General Servant. Elizabeth Francis, Visitor, 32. George Llewellyn, Brother, 37, Butcher.
1881 CENSUS	John Edwards, 72, Farmer . Jane Edwards, 57. Jane Edwards, 25; John James Edwards, 19. Ester Edwards, Niece, 31. Ellen Breeze, 17, Domestic Servant . Frederick Spencer, 16, Farm Servant Indoor.	John Batts, Head, 54, Innkeeper & Farmer. Jane Batts, 52. Fanny Batts, 23. Mary Batts, 17. William Batts, 10, Scholar.	Philip Llewellyn 49, Shopkeeper. Elizabeth Llewellyn, 50. Mary Ann Llewellyn, 18, Shop Assistant. Clara Llewellyn, 16; Alice Llewellyn, 14, Scholars Edmund Sheers, Brother In Law, 40, Assistant.
1891 CENSUS	John Edwards, 82, Farmer. Jane Edwards, 67. Jane Edwards, 35, Imbecile; James Edwards, Son, 29, Imbecile. Esther Edwards, Niece, 39; Lizzie Preece, 19, Domestic servants. Thomas Marshal, 15, Farm Servant.	John Batts, 64, Farmer and Inn Keeper. Jane Batts, 62. Fanny Batts, 32, Barmaid. William Batts, 20, Assistant farmer.	Margaret F. Magill, Nurse, 37, Orphans Superintendent, Annie James, 40, Parish Nurse, Esther Davies, 20, Domestic servant. Orphans: William H. Hall, 15, Arthur F. Hall, 10, Bertram L. Ray, 13, Hugh Vary, 12, John J. White11, James L. Saxby, 10, Thomas R. Ries, 9, Thomas A. Mason, 9, Henry A. Glen, 7.
1901 CENSUS	Jeremiah H. Edwards, 45, Farmer. Jessie Edwards, 44. Harris Edwards, 19, Articled clerk to lawyer William Edwards, 11; Rowland Edwards, 9; James Edwards, 7; Harold Edwards, 6; Mary Edwards, 3; Basil Edwards, 1.	Joseph Downing, 35, Innkeeper, farmer and coal merchant. Mary Downing, 36. Joseph Downing, 7; Edith E. Downing, 9; Matilda J. Downing, 3; Lillian M. Downing, 1. Fanny Batts, Sister-in-law, 40. George Davies, 16, Cattleman. Emily Errin, 22, General Servant, domestic.	Elizabeth Higginbotham, 45, Matron of Institution. Alice Gwinn, Nurse, 34, District Nurse (Sick nurse). Orphans: John Hall, 8, George E. Mason, 13, William S Clayden, 14, William Doyle, 14, William J Williams, 13, Harry M. Yates, 13, Percival T. Stephens, 12, Frederick Stephenson, 13, Frederick Felkin, 11, Albert Hardman, 11, John Hoboweigh, 11, Herbert V. Fielding, 12, Ernest Lloyd, 9, George Hall, 10 George Moore, 7, Charles Wilding, 7, John E. Thomas, 5.
③			
④			

① TITHE OWNER ② TITHE TENANT ③ 1918 SALE ④ PURCHASER

Streamside

The Cottage   Jessamine Cottage   Old Cottage/Alms House

	The Cottage	Jessamine Cottage	Alms House
1841 CENSUS	John Champion, 55, Excise Officer. Sarah Champion, 55. Martha Thomas, 15, Servant.	John Faulkner, 30, Tailor. Sophia Faulkner, 30. James Faulkner, 9; Frances Faulkner, 6; John Faulkner, 2.	
①	Samuel Wright	Samuel Wright	
②	Mrs Champion	John Faulkener	
1851 CENSUS	Unoccupied.	Edward Mason, 46, School Master, Parish Clerk Hannah Mason, 34, School mistress. Samuel Mason, 19. Sarah Elizabeth Mason, 15; Emma Mason, 9, Scholar. Hannah Mason, 3; Edward Mason, 12m.	James Bengough, 68, Sawyer. Hannah Bengough, 69, Midwife.
1861 CENSUS	Thomas Ross, 27, Saddler. Sarah Ross, 23. Margaret Ross, 3. Thomas Ross, 2. William Ross, 1 wk. John Ross, brother, 11, Scholar. Charles Seabourn, 14, Apprentice Saddler.	Edward, Mason, 56, Parish Clerk. Hannah Mason, 44. Hannah Mason, 13; Edward Mason, 11; William Mason, 8, Scholars. Lucy Mason, 2.	Mary Snead, widow, 80. Mary Surman, widow, 77.
1871 CENSUS	Samuel Palmer, 30, Saddler. Sarah Palmer, 45.	Hannah Mason, widow, 54, Seamstress. Lucy Mason, 12, Scholar.	Mary Snead, widow, 90, Annuitant. Mary Davies, widow, 79.
1881 CENSUS	John Combe, 28, Saddler. Jane Elizabeth Combe, 30.	Hannah Mason, 64, Formerly Seamstress. William John Mason, Grandson, 8, Scholar.	Mary Chance, 76. Ellen Whiting, Grand daughter, 9, Scholar. Eliza Bon..., 78.
1891 CENSUS	John, Southgate, 35, Sadler. Mary A. B. Southgate, 33. Ernest G. Southgate, 6; Sydney J. Southgate, 5, Scholars. Frederick C. Southgate, 6 m.	Hannah Mason, Widow, 74, Living on own means.	Ann Fleetwood, Widow, 75, Living on own means. Mary Saunders, Widow, 75, Living on own means.
1901 CENSUS	John Southgate, 44, Saddler. Mary A. Southgate, 42. Sidney J. Southgate, 15, Saddlers Apprentice. Frederick C. Southgate, 10. Ethel M. Southgate, 7.	Lucy Mason. 42, Schoolmistress Boarders; Louisa Ross, 14; Emily Ross, 12; Albert Ross, 8.	Diana Trumper Head widow, 69. Mary Beavan Head widow , 70.
③	John Southgate	Lucy Mason	Fanny Chase and Mary Beavan
④	Mr Parry	Mr Parry	Withdrawn from Sale

① **TITHE OWNER**   ② **TITHE TENANT**   ③ **1918 SALE**   ④ **PURCHASER**

Old Police House	Birdswood	7 Church Road	6 Church Road	Pilgrim Cottage

Old Police House	**Birdswood**	**7 Church Road**	**Pilgrim Cottage**
James Carver, 50, Carpenter. Ann Carver, 25. Thomas, Lunn, 50, Publican. George Sallery, 25, Schoolmaster.		Richard Langford, 30, Stonemason. Frances Langford, 25. William Langford, 1.	Ann Higgins, 65. John Higgins, 35, Shoemaker. Thomas Higgins, 30; John Jones, 25, Journeymen Shoemakers.
Thomas Perry		Robert Mutley	John Clayton.
James Carver		Richard Langford	Ann Higgins.
James Carver, 65, Carpenter master.		John Corbett, 44, Agricultural labourer. Ann Corbett, 35.	James Jenkins, 46, Journeyman Stone mason. Hellen Jenkins, 44, Laundress James Jenkins, 19, Journeyman Stone mason. Jane Jenkins, 13. Ellen Jenkins, 11. Mary A Jenkins, 6; Sophia Jenkins, 4, Scholars. Henry Jenkins, 13m.
James Carver, 75, Carpenter. John Corbett, lodger, 54, Proprietor of Houses. Anne Corbett, 45. Bessie M. Corbett, 2. William Corbett, nephew, 7, Scholar.		William Harper, 28, Spade tree turner. Ann Harper, 29. Sarah A. Harper, 1. George Halford, lodger, 19, Spade tree turner.	Elizabeth, Parker, widow, 80.
Anne Faulkener, widow, 54, Annuitant. Emma Agnes Carver, niece, 15.	William Wall, 37, Railway repair man. Margaret Wall, 29. Henry Wall, 6, Scholar. Jessie Wall, 4; Ada J. Wall, 1.	William Harper, 36, Spade tree turner. Ann Harper, 38. Sarah Ann Harper, 11; Lucy Cole Harper, 8, Scholars.	Thomas Lewis, 31, Carpenter. Elizabeth Lewis, 37. Frances Ann Lewis, 3.
William Harris, 60, Labourer Hannah Harris, 57 William Harris, 26, Miller Margaret Harris, 18, Dressmaker Bertie Harris, Grandson, 11months	William Wall, 49, Railway Labourer. Margaret Wall, 38. Ada Jane Wall, 11; Stella Mary Wall, 7; Margaret Ellen Wall, 4, Scholars. Mary Wall, Mother, widow, 78.	William Harper, 46, Spade Tree Maker. Ann Harper, 48. Sarah Anne Harper, 21, Dressmaker. Lucy C. Harper, 18.	Thomas Lewis, 41, Carpenter. Elizabeth Lewis, 47. Frances Ann Lewis, 13; William H.N. Lewis, 9, Scholars John Brown, Boarder, 15, Pupil Teachers
William, Harris, 70, Farm labourer. Hannah, Harris, 66. Margaret, Harris, 25, Dressmaker Herbert W Harris, Grandson, 10, Scholar. Boarders: George W Casswell, 23, Plumber. Henry G Harding, 23, Railway Signalman.	Margaret, Wall, Widow, 49, Living on own means, Stella Wall, 17 Maggie Wall, 14, Scholar. Wilfred James, Nephew, 7, Scholar. Boarders: Rosa M Bubb, 10, Scholar; William Little, 19, Groom; John Adams, 61, Spade Tree Maker.	William, Harper, 57, Spade Tree Maker. Annie Harper, 57. Lucy C. Harper, 28, Dressmaker. Mary A. Burke, Visitor, 25, Living on own means.	Elizabeth Lewis, Widow, 59, Housekeeper Frances Lewis, 28 William H. Lewis, 19, Carpenter. Boarders: Robert Lingwood, 13, Scholar; George R Powell, 21, Railway porter; William H Pickford, 17, Railway clerk.
Hannah Harries, widow, 76 William Harries, 46, Game Keeper.	Margaret Wall, widow, 59 Living on own means, Margaret E. Wall, 24. Elizabeth Wall, Grand daughter, 6. James Adams, Boarder, 71, Spade Tree Turner.	William Harper, widower, 67, Spade Tree turner. Lucy C. Harper, 38, dressmaker	William Lewis, 29, Carpenter. Ellen Lewis, 31. Arthur T. Lewis, 4; Elizabeth F. Lewis, 3; Ellen W. Lewis, 2.
William Harris William Morris		Lucy Harper	Constabulary
Mr Preece		Mr. Philpin	Mr. Harris

5 Church Road	4	3	2	1 Church Road

5 Church Road	4 Church Road	3 Church Road	2 Church Road	1 Church Road
Elizabeth Watkins, 80, Pauper.	Margaret Herring, 55, Agricultural Labourer. Ann Morris, 15.	James Wall, 35, Agricultural Labourer. Mary Wall, 35. James Wall, 35. Ann Wall, 1.	William Page, 25, Painter and Glazier. Mary Page, 20. Frederic Page, 1. Jane Page, 7m.	Hannah Ciswell, 60, Agricultural Labourer. Jane Ciswell, 20, Agricultural Labourer. William Ciswell, 10. James Hughes, 25, Agricultural Labourer.
Thomas Jones.	Thomas Jones.	Revd Rice Price	Revd Rice Price.	Revd Rice Price.
Elizabeth Watkins.	Samuel Vaughan.	James Jones	William Lloyd.	William Page.
William Jones, 26, Journeyman Miller . Mary Jones, 23, Milliner.	Elizabeth Jones, 45, Charwoman. Sarah Jones, 20, seamstress. John Jones, 18, Agricultural labourer. Edwin Jones, 11, Scholar. Eliza Jones, 8; Joseph Jones, 3; Hannah Jones, 7m.	John Weaver, 48, Journeyman Mason. Elizabeth Weaver, 47. Fanny Weaver, 10, Scholar. Martha Williams, lodger, 77.	William Bomfry, 45, Agricultural labourer; Elizabeth Bomfry, 40, Charwoman. Eliza Bomfry, 20; Ellen Bomfry, 19, General servants. Priscilla Bomfry, 9, Scholar. Elizabeth Morgan, lodger, 70, Travelling hawker. Martha Williams, 68, Pauper on parish relief.	William Page, 38, Plumber and Glazier. Mary Page, 35, seamstress. Frederick Page, 11; Jane Ann Page, 10; Mary Agnes Page, 8; Emma Page, 5, Scholars. William Page, 3; Leonard Page, 12m, at home.
Elizabeth Morgan, widow, 79, Formerly a hawker. Mary Ford, lodger, 37, Washerwoman. Lodgers: Eliza Ford, 10; Alice Ford, 4, Scholars; George Ford, 2.	James Jones, 33, Police Officer. Jane Jones, 29. William Jones, 7; Alice Jones, 5, Scholars. Mary F Jones, 2; Emma Jones, 11m.	James Saunders, 37, Agricultural labourer. Mary Saunders, 36. Thomas Saunders, 11, Scholar. Elizabeth Saunders, 2; James Saunders, 6. Lodgers: John Pugh, 48; James Jones, 22, Agricultural Labourers.	William Jenkins, 37, Gardener. Mary Jenkins, 36, Gardener's wife. Letitia Jenkins, 7; Elizabeth Jenkins, 5, Scholar.	Thomas Price, 69, Agricultural labourer. Elizabeth Price, 34, Dressmaker. Francis Evans, lodger, 44, Shoemaker.
Richard Edwards, 37, Police Sergeant; Sarah Edwards, 33, Police sergeants Wife. Andrew Edwards, 11; Henry James Edwards, 9; Emily S. Edwards, 6, Scholars; Richard Edwards, 3; Eva Mary Edwards, 1; William Stott, widower, 67, Carpenter.	John Delahay, 35, Railway Labourer. Susan Delahay, 32; Emily Delahay, 4; Susan Delahay, 2. Theodocia Delahay, Mother, widow, 70.	Thomas Spencer, 46, Agricultural labourer; Mary Spencer, 45. Thomas Spencer, 20; Edward Spencer, 14, Agricultural labourers. Farringdon Spencer, 11; Frederick Spencer, 8. Elizabeth Spencer, 6; Jane Spencer, 4.	James Seabourne, 68, Labourer. Elizabeth Seabourne, 52. William Price, 22, Labourer. Catherine Walters, Boarder, 5, Scholar.	Elizabeth Walters, widow, 57, Charwoman. Elizabeth Walters, Grand daughter, 2. Lodgers: Jane Morris, widow, 47; Ann Jenkins, widow, 64.
Benjamin Lewis, 47, Police Sergeant. Maud Lewis, 18, Domestic Servant. Auldah Lewis, 16, Formerly In A Drapers Shop. Agnes Lewis, 14, Scholar. Lavinia Lewis, 4.	Esther Gummer, Widow, 55, Housekeeper. Joseph Gummer, Brother, 62; Richard Roberts, Boarder, 60, General Labourers. Boarders: Matilda, Hammonds, 6; Ellen M Hayles, 5, Scholars.	Thomas Spencer 57, Farm Labourer. Mary Spencer, 56. Edward Spencer, 22, Farm Labourer. Jane Spencer, 13, Scholar.	James Seaborne, 78, (No Occupation) Elizabeth Seaborne, 63 Boarders: Victor Samuel Shackstone, 2, Nurse Child; William Jones, widower, 77.	Elizabeth Walters, widow, 67, Nurse. Elizabeth Walters, Grand daughter, 13, Scholar. Jane Morris, Lodger, widow, 57
Benjamin Lewis, 58, Police Sergeant. Eliza A. Lewis, 53. Helen L. Lewis, 14, Scholar. Mary A. Morgan, Boarder, 11, Scholar.	Esther Gummer, Widow, 55, Housekeeper. Joseph Gummer, Brother, 62, General Labourer, Boarders: Richard Roberts, 60, General Labourer; Matilda Hammonds, 6; Ellen M, Hayles, 5, Scholar.	William Davies, 50, General Labourer Fanny Davies, 47 Fanny M Davies, 12; Emily L Davies, 9; Alice M Davies, 4, Scholars.	William Price, 46, Agricultural labourer, Mary Ann Price, 46, Domestic servant, Victor S Strachan, Nephew, 12, Scholar.	Unoccupied
Alfred Nicholas, 38 Railway Guard. Ellen Nicholas, 36; Edith Nicholas, 9; Robert Nicholas, 7; Ellen Nicholas, 4; William Nicholas, 2; John Weston Boarder, 17, Groom.	Elizabeth Williams, widow, 57, Monthly Nurse. Mary E Williams Grand daughter, 13 Nurse children: Lily Lamacroft, 12; Mary Hughes, 6; May Hughes, 4.	William Davies, 60 Ordinary labourer. Fanny Davies, 57. William Davies, 24 Grocers Assistant. Alice Davies, 14.	No record found.	Henry Smith, 56, Butcher. Lambert Smith, 19, Butcher. Sophia A. Smith, 15.
Alfred Nicholas	Martha Bubb	Fanny Davies	John Townsend.	Lambert Smith.
Mr. Povey	Mr. Povey	Mr Tebb	Mr. Tebb.	Mr. Tebb.

New Inn

Although this inn was not copyhold many of the meetings of the court were held there. These entries provide a series of 'snapshots' of the tenants or owners:

1748. John Crump, son and heir of John Crump late of The Steps, Eardisley, Gentleman, deceased.

1767. Surrendered to Richard Coke by Sarah Ball of Hereford, widow.

1767. House called The Steps in possession of Richard Coke, Clerk,

1785. At the House of Joseph Winter called the New Inn.

1786. At the New Inn, home of Edward Turner.

1792. House of Henry Watkins known as the Steps Inn.

1795. At the home of Robert Morris, "the New Inn then called The Steps"

1797. At The Steps, house of Robert Morris.

1832. The Steps, once in possession of Thomas Hall, glover, since of Thomas Farr once in possession of Richard Coke and now Thomas Farr.

1841. Tithe - owned by Rev George Coke, occupied by John Baker.

1845. Held at New Inn home of John Baker.

1847. Court Leet held at New Inn. Thomas Whitehouse.

1851. Court Leet at New Inn home of William Bryan.

1853. At the New Inn, home of William Bryan.

1884. Court Leet of Sophia Perry-Herrick at New Inn in occupation of John Batts.

The early name "the Steps" may well have referred to a time when the building was simply a farm house. The changing of name seems to have occurred in the early 19th century, but the original name seems to have persisted, and it was even remembered by older village residents in this century. The Inn always had farming links, and many of the landlords are described as farmers as well as innkeepers. There used to be a range of outbuildings behind the main building.

As with the Tram, the New Inn performed an important function as a focus and meeting place for village societies – a function it retains to the present day. One of the earliest, The Eardisley Friendly Society, adopted a formidable 24-page set of rules on the 1st January, 1798.

That it shall be the rule of this Society that every person who shall offer himself a Member thereof shall be a man of sober and peaceable life and conversation.

Meetings shall be held every four weeks at the New Inn kept by Robert Morris on a Saturday... when 10d. shall be paid to the box and 2d. spent... The stewards will order a small cup or tumbler with the first carriage of ale, and members drink from this only, under a fine of 2d.

A Box shall be provided with three locks and three different keys for the purpose of depositing and keeping money ... the Landlord to keep one key, and the Stewards one key each.

There shall be a feast ... upon the 4th June, unless it happen on a Sunday or Wednesday. Members to walk to church with oak leaves in their hats, and pay 2/- for their dinner ... to include a quart of ale.

These rules were printed in 1818 when Francis Coke and Thomas Harris were appointed trustees, John Harris Treasurer, Omwell Lloyd Secretary and John Prothero and James Cartwright Stewards.

The benefits were the payment of 6/- weekly for six months during illness if the funds amounted to £50 0s 0d, or 3/- for life if incurable. These sums were subject to two years' previous membership. After twenty years members were to have £3 35 0d if funds were not reduced to £200 0s 0d. At the death of a member 40/- was contributed towards the funeral, eight others having to attend this and to carry the coffin under fine of 1/-.

Later the "Royal Oak Club" met at New Inn. Its rules were first certified on the 18th October 1825. Another friendly society, the Ancient Order of Druids Benefit Club, also met here.

June 15th was fixed for the holiday of the benefit society which has had a Branch in this Parish for about 20 years, being introduced here by the late honoured Vicar, Revd W. St. Leger Oldworth, when the old club had broken up.

There was a strong muster of members, 63 out of a total number of 88 when the service in Church took place at 12.15.

After walking in procession to the Rectory, Parton, the Castle and Upper House, the Members of the club assembled for dinner at the New Inn, where Mr and Mrs Bates had prepared a most excellent repast. The room was well filled, as many visitors and friends to the Society dined with them. The Rector occupied the chair, Mr Vaughan the vice-chair.

Tea was prepared at the schoolroom by the Rector and Mrs Palmer for the Members wives and friends, each Member having a ticket to dispose of. By this time the weather had cleared up and the long procession coming through the village with its handsome new banner had a striking appearance. The band of the Hay volunteers was in attendance and played during the day.

EARDISLEY PARISH MAGAZINE JULY 1883

Winter made its appearance early in December and on the night of 12th December there were exceptionally heavy snow-falls along the Border, especially on the Radnor Hills and around Knighton. Just around 9.00am on the following morning fire broke out in the New Inn and rapidly spread in the strong wind. A message was sent on the Telegraph to the Kington and Hay Fire Brigades and in the meantime everyone came to help fight the fire and remove the furniture and animals to places of safety. The new Hay Steam Fire

Engine arrived at l0.45am, by which time the main building was burning fiercely and volunteers were trying to remove parts of the Brewhouse roof to prevent the fire destroying that as well.

A calf was burned to death in the cowshed and the fire drove the rescuers out of two rooms before they could take out the furniture. It took until around 3.30pm before the fire was brought under control and by that time there were only a few walls left standing to mark the spot.

The Inn belonged to the Newport Estate at this time and fortunately for them it was insured, but for the Downing family at the Inn it meant that their Christmas was not the one they would have wished for, even though the villagers did everything they could for them.

DAVID GORVETT. 'DAWN OF DAY EARDISLEY IN 1901'

There was the big wall where the New Inn is, where the car park is today. Farm people, labourers, maids – all the big houses, Bollingham, Lemore even the Rectory, Parton Farm, they all had maids – and they would stand against the wall if they wanted a new job. People would go and interview them. If they decided they liked the person they would give them a shilling. That was their bond that they had to go and work for them. Farm hands, everybody would be there.

LILLIAN BARON

In 1909 the New Inn was still part of the Newport Estate and let to Mrs Downing on an annual rent of £60.

By this time Mr and Mrs Charley Jones had the New Inn. Mrs Charley Jones was a very good pianist but she was rather flamboyant in her actions. She used to play for children's concerts or sometimes after Church on a Saint's day or something, she would play, and there was a great show physical playing on the keyboard. And once her ring flew off and she lost it in the hall. My father came in because we had finished our little show and we were ushered off home, and my father came in and said, 'You children, tomorrow you're to go into the hall and Mrs Jones has lost a valuable ring'. Of course we went to find this and I found it, it didn't mean anything to me that it was a diamond, it was a stone to me! I went across to the New Inn and there was a side door into the garden and that used to be the dining room. People who came to the New Inn had meals there, what is now the post office was her little private sitting room. I was taken through into the dining room and she was so delighted to get her ring back she gave me 6d, Oh my goodness 6d! Go and find another ring tomorrow! Yes!

JOAN WILLIAMS

Until his death in 1969 the licensee was Mr. Reg. Jones who was also the Rector's churchwarden and secretary of the local branch of the British Legion. It is here that the Legion have their headquarters. In the early 70's the name of the inn was changed to "The Mountie" and several alterations were carried out. The licensee is now Mr. D. Harvey who is Mr. Jones's son-in-law. In the darts world they go one better than the Tram because they also have a ladies team.

WI SCRAPBOOK 1977

The New Inn after the fire in 1901. Mrs Downing stands in the doorway.

51

The Holme

This is probably the most significant surviving timber-framed medieval hall house in Eardisley. Made from timber felled in the winter of 1442, it is likely to have been built during 1443. The hall range is laid out alongside the Almeley road with the cross-wing solar range set parallel to the main road through the village. The large cross-wing, now underbuilt, was originally jettied at first floor level on both the west and north elevations. There is a later, single-bay extension at the south end. The bargeboards on the north gable are decorated with cusped, blind arcading. At first floor level in the cross-wing there was a great chamber measuring 20ft square although this is now subdivided by a timber-framed partition.

The hall range contains heavily smoke-blackened timbers in the roof, indicative of an open fire on a central hearth. There are pairs of curved wind braces in each half bay and two arch-braced trusses over the hall. There is a later, inserted ceiling. The existing front door is on the line of the original cross passage through the lower end of the hall. The service accommodation (buttery and pantry) has been rebuilt in brick.

With a floor area of about 440 sq. ft., the hall is the third largest in the village, exceeded only by The Forge and 1–3 Church Road.

Both the cross-wing and hall ranges were sampled for tree-ring dating and gave a felling date for the timber of winter 1442 which means that the building was almost certainly erected during 1443.

Before 1820 this house was in multiple ownership.

The first consisted of four rooms on the highway side of the building, with 'the Clay Chamber and a room over the shop', occupied before 1729 by Elizabeth Davies. In that year William Holdes took possession, passing it on to his children Alice and Susannah Houlds in 1731.

Susannah (Susan) married Peter Symmonds and they were admitted to the house in 1777. They had a child Mary, who went on to marry Samuel Price in 1772 and to have a son William, who became a linen draper in Ironmonger Lane, London.

The parish records in Eardisley record the death of a Mary Price in 1776, and Samuel Price marrying Bridget Lewis later in the same year.

The second part of the house was described as consisting of 'a room called the Hall, another called the Kiln or Killing Room and the Upper Rooms from the Quining or Cross sill or style of the other part of the said House, also an alley adjoining, also a building called the Penthouse and a small fold with pigscott'

Sarah Powell left the house to her daughter Alice (and her husband William Bromley) and her son Thomas (and his wife Elinor) in 1735.

The property was to pass to Thomas Powell for his life and then on to William Bromley. Bromley was a watchmaker in Shrewsbury and when he died in 1744 he named his sister Elizabeth and her husband George Hopton as his heirs. They sold their interest to Thomas Powell in 1769. Thomas was a periwig maker, and business must have been slow because he immediately mortgaged the property to Phillip Taylor of Parton for £10.

In 1777 Taylor sold the property to James Whitney. When he died in 1803 his eldest son James Whitney, a surgeon in Henley, inherited and sold to Samuel and Bridget Price.

The third part was described as a 'half burgage, a house taken out of another', and was behind the other houses. Thomas Powell mortgaged the property to Alice Houlds for £15 in 1755 to be redeemed on the 28th April 1758. Just over a year after taking out the mortgage Powell transferred his interest to Alice's sister Mary Symonds [sic]. In 1777 Mary took the house on trust for her 4 year old son William Price.

In addition to the main buildings there was 'barn, pigscott, fold and small hopyard' to the west of the house was a which passed on the death of Thomas Powell in 1757 to Nicholas Everall of Ruttling Hope, Salop. In 1787 the property passed to Thomas Everall; the tenant was John Evans, and he was still there in 1820 when Thomas sold to Samuel and Bridget Price and Joseph Price for £84.

By 1820 Samuel and Bridget had consolidated the property and were running a thriving shop in a prime position on the edge of the market square.

Samuel had children by both his wives, and probably in an attempt to prevent conflict an arrangement was entered into where one of their children, William, paid his half-brother, Joseph, a haberdasher now living in London, a total of £118 as a remainder or reversion of any benefits expected on the 'four rooms' and the barn on the death of his parents. Joseph retained the benefits on the 'Hall' section.

William Price was living in Aldermanbury in 1820, working as a warehouseman, and intended to marry Elizabeth Powles of Hereford. He surrendered the reversion in trust to John Powles and Daniel Pearce to provide an independent income for his intended wife. It would revert to William if Elizabeth died.

William Price died in Eardisley in 1822, and Elizabeth in 1836, so by the time of the Tithe apportionment John Powles had inherited the property and Phillip Llewellyn, a shopkeeper, was his tenant. Phillip handed the shop on to his son in the 1850s, and he continued there until about 1885.

In 1885 Mrs C S Palmer, wife of Canon Palmer, founded a home for 20 orphan boys in the house. Initially by voluntary subscriptions control was taken over by the Hereford Board of Guardians in 1908.

The census lists the birthplace of the boys. While some were local, from Kington or Whitney, only one is recorded as being born in Eardisley. The majority came from much further afield, from Cheshire, London, Oxford, Dorset, Middlesex, Hampshire and Sussex.

The boys' home, I don't remember much about the boys that were there, before my time. I remember that four boys had been drowned in the river. It was before my time but people still used to talk about it.

MARY PRICE

52

Frederick Harrison, Boys' Home, Eardisley, Died Sept 20th 1904 Aged 7

In Memory of George Yates, Aged 13. Sydney Dicker, Aged 11, Stanley Rice, Aged 13.

Loved Children Of The Boys Home, Eardisley. Drowned In The Wye, Sept 10th 1898.

INSCRIPTION ON GRAVESTONE,
EARDISLEY CHURCHYARD

Wilfred Burns was born in 1917 in Eardisley where his parents were master and matron of the boys' home. As a teenager, he was relief organist in the diocese of Hereford and played the Cathedral organ. In 1936 he joined the regular Army as a bandsman. After the war he worked for music publishers and at Elstree studios before becoming a freelance film composer and musical director. He wrote the theme of the 1960s game show 'Truth or Consequences', and among the films for which he composed music are Adolf Hitler - My Part in His Downfall (1972), Dad's Army (1971), and Till Death Us Do Part (1969). He died in 1990.

THE INTERNET'S COMPOSERS
AND LYRICISTS DATABASE

Mr. Vaughan, the churchwarden, was one of the village elders whose butcher business had failed in the depression and had relocated to the Holme and ran it as a guest house for the few fishermen that were able to visit during the salmon run. One of his daughters was a commissioned officer in WAAF and always arrived on leave looking very smart.

BRIAN JONES

The Vaughans went there after that, and they used to have salmon fishing people there, I knew there were three lots, all gentry, or people that had come to money. Mr Lugar bought the Holme when they went broke or it was closed then. But Nurse Gwynn, she was the matron of the boys' school, and then she went as a housekeeper to a man called Mr Foster, and he had three children and he had the sawmill. It must have been at the wharf.

LILLIAN BARRON

In Honoured Memory Of Arthur William Vaughan, Who Served Faithfully as Churchwarden and in Many Capacities In The Parish Of Eardisley For 44 Years 1903-1944. Died November 6th 1944 R.I.P.

MEMORIAL, EARDISLEY CHURCH

Bank House and Vine House

Although these houses are not linked structurally they were in common ownership for over 150 years and are therefore listed together.

Hidden behind the modern façade of Bank House is an unusual two-storey, three-bay timber-framed building of high quality. Now underbuilt, the first floor was originally jettied along the street front. The first-floor rooms, each with an intermediate truss across the middle, were all open to the ridge of a roof that was, and still is, richly decorated with a total of 25 cusped wind braces. It was probably built in the second half of the 15th century. A large chimney stack at the north end is a later addition.

For a number of reasons this is a building that does not fit into the normal pattern of domestic accommodation and it may be appropriate to consider whether it served a commercial function.

The primary structure of Vine House is a timber frame possibly of late 17th or early 18th century date. Later alterations include raising the height of the roof to create more headroom at first floor level and re-facing the front in brick.

Several factors combine to make reconstructing the ownership of these properties difficult. There have been changes in the way the buildings were occupied as parts were sold and let, and there is a lack of consistency in some of the records as they failed to keep pace with the changes of tenants. The way in which the buildings have been divided may also have changed. The houses marked on the Tithe map are very difficult to interpret, and the boundaries marked do not seem to correspond with buildings known to be there at the time.

The early entries in the manorial record for Bank House property are fragmentary. In 1737 the property was granted to a parson, Joseph Hall and his wife Alice and daughter Martha, having recently been occupied by Cornelius Bowen. There is no other mention of any of these persons anywhere else in the records, and no further mention of the property until 1767 when it was occupied by George Lloyd and passed from Mansell Powell, the Lord of the Manor, to John Morris a butcher.

In 1748 Vine House was occupied by Charles and Sarah Powell and described as a 'dwelling house, hopyard and garden'. The owner was William Godsall, and he had recently inherited it from his father Thomas.

There is an unbroken sequence of ownership coming down to Thomas Godsall, but the description of the property in these early transactions differs from the one used after 1750. However there are enough consistent facts across these dates to feel confident only one property was involved, and the changes may be due to another piece of land or part of a building being consolidated into this piece.

Before 1733 the house was rented to James Elcocks. Thomas Godsall acquired the property from Charles and Sarah Powell, and Frances Baskerville in 1737. Sarah had acquired part of the property in 1733 from Francis and Rowland Prees. They were the sons of Rowland Prees, and it is not known if Sarah was his daughter, but this seems likely. Frances Baskerville may have provided a mortgage or loan for this transaction. Francis Baskerville is described as a spinster; she was Phillippa Kent's sister (see Arboyne House). There is no evidence that she ever lived in the house.

In 1749 Thomas Godsall surrendered the house to Thomas Cook of Kinnersley. Charles and Sarah Powell still had an interest in the property, as their name appears on the roll when Cooke sold the property to John Morris a butcher from Kington and his wife Mary in 1755.

John Morris now owned both properties, and they would remain linked by ownership for the next 150 years.

George Lloyd lived in Bank House and Morris may have lived in Vine House when he sold both houses to Walter Taylor in 1771. By 1787 William Higgins lived in Bank House when the properties were mortgaged to James Lloyd Harris, an attorney, for £80 a piece.

Walter Taylor's occupation was not listed, but he was probably a butcher, as that was the trade of his son William Taylor who inherited the properties in 1816. William died intestate in 1830, and when his wife Mary died three years later she left the property in her will to her brothers-in-law James and Walter Taylor of London, butchers, and her brother James Connop of Welson, a farmer. They sold the houses three years later for £480 to Thomas Mainwaring Harris. Harris was a farmer who owned property and rented land in the parish. His son Thomas was a butcher and he moved into the house. The census of 1841 records that he employed James Connop's son, William, as an apprentice.

There is a gap in the records until 1861 when both properties were granted to John Vaughan; he had already lived in Vine House for over 10 years as a tenant. His son Arthur William Vaughan inherited in 1887.

At the turn of the century Vine House was rented by John Page and run as a shop and post office. In 1901 he was declared bankrupt owing £284 15s 5d. At his examination at Leominster on 13th May, he did not appear personally and the Receiver was told that he was in South Africa, having enlisted in the Army and been posted there in the fight against the Boers. Later in the year his creditors were to receive a final dividend of 6/8d in the pound. Mr George Vale stepped in and looked after the postal affairs until the end of the year.

December was to be a sad month for the Tram as it saw the death of the landlord, Mr Baird, a fact which was noted at a public Dinner at the New Inn on 22nd in honour of Mr G Vale who had come to the rescue of the village early in the year when the Postmaster had left.

It would seem that the idea of the dinner and a presentation of an inkstand to Mr Vale came from a group of Almeley men, who wanted to recognise the contribution that this 'straightforward and upright' man had made to their village as Parish Councillor and member of the School Board.

Apparently the Eardisley men present were not entirely aware of all this and so, during the evening Mr Edwards of Upper House Farm, opened an Instant Presentation Fund! It is not clear what this resulted in, or whether a present for Mr and Mrs Vale was bought in time before they left to start another business in the booming seaside resort of Southend by Sea. As it happened this was to be the last special occasion to be held at the New Inn, but no one could know this on this evening.

DAVID GORVETT. 'DAWN OF DAY. EARDISLEY IN 1901'

In 1912 Vaughan sold to the houses to Alice Jay for £750. The records are incomplete, but it seems this property was part of the mortgage described for the Central Stores in 1920. At some time Ellen Baird acquired the properties, selling to Arthur Robert Wynne, butcher, for £1,400 in 1927. Robert Wynne became a butcher in Eardisley soon after the 1914-1918 war. He lived in Vine House; his shop was in the northern part of the building.

In 1937 Robert Wynne had one van and a horse and cart. He employed two qualified cutters, Mr Jim Prime and Mr Bufton, plus two young boys who lived in. In 1939 Mr Frank Wynne (brother of Bob) came from South Wales to replace Mr Bufton who had been called up. He lived at Hurstley, Kinnersley from 1940 before moving to Bank House Eardisley in 1953. Also Mr Tom Penny did a Saturday round (he

The Eardisley Post Office at Vine House, about 1901

was a postman). *About 1937 a butcher in Staunton-on-Wye went bankrupt. Bob Wynne took over his business which enabled him to have further vans and expand his business.*

During the Second World War he had 3 vans delivering meat when it was rationed. This was before the days of freezers and supermarkets. He retired in 1957 or 1958 when Peter Preece took over.

DORIS WEALE

Before the Abattoir was built the slaughter house was on the side of the street. The animals were unloaded by the side of the street and they were killed in a bit farther on.

GLEN PROBERT

Bob Wynne also owned Bank House; one downstairs room was used by Barclays Bank. Every Friday a Bank Clerk and his assistant would arrive by the morning train from Hay-on-Wye with a suitcase containing money and papers and open the Bank at 10.00 a.m. The Bank closed at 3.00 p.m. giving the staff time to pack their suitcase and take it down to the Railway Station in time to catch the 4.30 p.m. train back to Hay-on-Wye. This ceased on the 25th September 1992.

There was a Bank here; it came once a week from Hay-on-Wye, it came to Bank House. When that stopped coming that's when the businesses stopped in Eardisley, the Butcher, because it bought people into the village for the Bank.

MURIEL FENTON

In 1958 when Mr. Preece took over from Mr. Bob Wynne this was just a small family butcher but over the years this has been extended and now Mr. Preece supplies Wholesale meat to butchers over a wide area. He also supplies many hotels and restaurants transporting meat to Liverpool and other far flung areas. As well as extending the abattoir a new butchers shop has been built next door to the old one and from here the business of delivering the meat to the surrounding villages is carried on.

WI SCRAPBOOK 1965

Stoneleigh

This stone-fronted house was probably built in the late 18th or early 19th century. Between 1826 and 1918 the owners of this property also owned the Old Parsonage.

In the 1870s the house was occupied by William Tantram and his family before they moved to Northway. Since then it has been continually occupied by members of the same family. In the 1880s William Parsons moved there with his wife Sarah. He was a labourer and his wife ran a laundry. In the Estate Sale the house consisted of 'six Rooms, Pantry and Wash House with side entrance leading to a Garden in the rear in which is a Detached Laundry and Wood Shed, a Detached Piggery and a Pump... The Washing Copper and Furnace belong to the Tenant.' The annual rent was £6 10s. William Parsons bought it for £175.

Miss Parsons lived next door to the Central Stores and ran a laundry, her sister and brother-in-law lived in the Institute House and they were the caretakers of the Hall for many years.

GLEN PROBERT

Central Stores

The first record of this building changing hands is in 1806 when the property was sold to John Harper, a 35-year-old blacksmith from Eardisley, and his wife Ann.

The vendors give a clue to the history of ownership. They were James Protheroe and his sister Elizabeth and her husband William Buitt, and mortgagees Thomas and Judith Bird. Judith Bird's maiden name was Preece, and she provided a mortgage to Samuel Protherough for the Knapp House in 1769. James and Elizabeth Protheroe were the heirs of Samuel Protheroe, so this house was probably also owned by the Protheroe family.

At the time of the sale in 1806 the occupant was Thomas Powell, and before him it had been John Price.

The Harpers converted the tenement to two dwellings, living in one half and renting the other to Mary Feares, a dressmaker. By 1826 they had mortgaged the property to William Downes for £200. This mortgage was redeemed by two gentlemen, Benjamin Coates of Eyton Lodge, and John Colebatch of Brighthelmstone (Brighton) as trustees of a deed of settlement made in 1805 of John Griffiths and Letitia Crump. What their interest in the property was is not known.

Mary Feares was replaced as tenant by Thomas Watkins a saddler, and later by James Powell a tailor. The mortgage was probably redeemed, because the Harpers continued to live in the house until Ann died aged 87 in 1855 and John died aged 90 in 1860. The house passed to their grandson John Harper in 1861 he used the whole property to run a grocery and baking business and operate the village post office.

Two children stand outside the Stores in the 1890s.

There was a Bakehouse there, always had bread and cakes. On the right-hand side as you went through the door there was the post office part of the shop. They used to sell material, so the old folks told me, for aprons and things like that, coarse things, calico. And outside they would have brushes and brooms and buckets and spades, forks hanging at the side of the window, the top window in particular.

LILLIAN BARRON

In 1891, and at the age of 68, John sold the business to a member of the family, Rosa Mary Vale, for £400. Rosa's maiden name was Vaughan, and she had grown up virtually next door at Vine House, and her husband George Vale was John Harper's nephew.

In 1901 the old Stores was burnt to the ground. The property was rebuilt, and Harley Jay moved into the new building, his father John Jay of Arboyne House providing security.

Mr Jordan, who lived at Hobby Lyons, was baker for the people that had the shop…during the first war people name of Clements lived there for a short time, or it didn't seem to me to be very long.

Mr Jay then had the bakery, and Uncle Reg. that brought me up he was master baker and he opened five bake houses for the Cooperative Stores in South Wales and he had many men working under him but then Mr Jay in Eardisley sent us a telegram … and it just said 'Baker Wanted - old home vacant'. That's how we came back to Eardisley. That's before the estate was sold up in 1918. We came from Blackwood, left the Cooperative, he was there till he finished.

Down at the place where Harley Jay went to, because he worked for his father at first, then he got married and went to the other shop. I think the people that lived there before were named Powell; I don't know anything about them. They were a general store; they sold buckets and all sorts of things.

My uncle was up at half past 4 to light the fires, then he

The rebuilt Stores with Harley Jay's name above the door. The sign on the western side of the street announces the Refreshment Rooms of the Eardisley Church Institute.

wouldn't come home for breakfast, he would have that down there, and he came home for lunch, then he went back about 2 or quarter past. He came home for tea about half past 4, and he would go back again at half past 6, and he would be there until half past 8 or 9 o'clock making the dough for the first lot of bread to come out in the morning. The next morning at half past 4 he would be up, straight down to light the fires.

They made hand mixed bread, and they made batch cakes – flat loaves 3 or 4 inches thick and they were a shilling I think, in the days when I was going to school. That was in Jay's time. The old oven was there, I think uncle used to put in 150, or perhaps 250, loaves at a time. They were mixed by hand, weighed by hand, moulded by hand and remoulded by hand! Cottage loaves, Swansea loaves – a loaf about 6 inches across with another a bit smaller of the top – you stuck your thumb in the middle of it. All the loaves were the same weight, it had to be, the inspectors would come round.

They used to do cakes, at Easter time he used to make literally thousands of hot cross buns, and because I wasn't going to school at the time, on Friday we broke up school in the morning, I was allowed to stay up. Friday night you go and put the crosses on the buns, on the troughs, there would be troughs right along the Bakehouse, and my mum used to help him. Those had to be weighed. And they were put onto big sheets of tin, and I used to along with a little wooded cross, not like today with a pastry on it, it was a wooden cross stamped onto it and then they were brushed with sugar and water. I remember doing those quite well.

One daughter from Jay's she would come with me and people in the village would leave their kitchen window open and we would put the buns in the windows for them. I was allowed to stay up to 12 or 1 o'clock. My uncle would go straight through the day on the Thursday baking all through the night and Friday morning and finish about lunchtime on Good Friday. The people were still delivering the hot cross buns.

LILLIAN BARRON

Later, Harley Jay also bought Bank House and Vine House, completing a near family monopoly on Eardisley Stores. But this was not to last. On the 18th August 1908 John Jay and Harley Jay were adjudged bankrupts at the County Court of Hereford at Leominster. The fault lay with the father, but their interests were too closely linked for the son to escape, and they had to sell their house in Hobby Lyons. In 1920 Alice, Harley Jay's widow, mortgaged her remaining property to Charles Philpotts of Parsonage Farm, George Pritchard of Spond, and William Cartwright for £600. Alice Jay in turn went bankrupt in1922 and the property passed to the mortgagees. George Triffit had been renting it for some time, and he purchased it in 1926.

Jays the shop, Central Stores, they had a waggonette and a tub. The waggonette could carry six people, three each side, one could sit up with the driver in the front, and that was a shilling to go from the station to where ever. Usually it was one of the drivers who took the carts out delivering the groceries, or Uncle on Sundays if he had a batch of bread and he had 30 or 40 minutes he would go out. It was a stone road and you could hear the clip-clop as the horse came up the road.

The two grocer's shops they would deliver and take an order for the next week … they would pay for their goods when the next lot was delivered, that's how they used to do it, but it was always horses and carts. I remember the first van that was brought to Eardisley by Mr Triffit. I was about 11 or 12 I suppose. (1922-24)

LILLIAN BARRON

As a treat I sometimes was given a penny halfpenny or tuppence to buy a fresh baked batch loaf and a piece of cheese from Triffit's shop where Eardisley stores is now. Sometimes I would have enough money to buy some toffees and they were weighed sometimes by Mr Triffitt who would cut a toffee in half to give the exact weight.

JOHN MORRIS

During the winter of 1947 the snow came in January and stayed until May. There was a tremendous fall of snow and everything was at a standstill. To help the local butcher and grocer Robert Preece from Upper House did the Almeley Lyonshall route and I did the Kinnersley and Norton Canon and Sarnesfield Oak run. The last trip I did was from Eardisley shop, George Triffitt's. We loaded the bread and the meat from Mr Wynne's and with Jim Prime and Fred Boyce we started off on our round through Willersley to Winforton, up as far as the Rhydspence, we made our way back and tried to get up to Brilley. We got as far as Welsh Wood and we were beaten by the depth of snow, which was as high as the telegraph poles on the side of the road. We stopped by Minton's and had our cup of tea and sandwiches and reversed back to Millhalf because we couldn't turn round, and then went back and delivered the bread and meat in sacks and leaving it at the nearest household. We finished up at Whitney Court and Captain Hope gave me permission to drive the tractor and trailer down the back drive as he thought it was too dangerous to go by the main road. We got back to Eardisley at 9 o'clock that evening.

DENIS LAYTON

The Central Stores was a grocer's shop and bakery run by Mr George Triffitt. He occupied the house with his wife. Her two nephews Doug and Bert Jones were employed here as was Godfrey Davies, the nephew of Mr and Mrs Booth, when he was old enough. Godfrey eventually took over the business.

BILL BRIERLEY

In 1953 … the Central Stores was run by Mr. D. Jones in partnership with Mr. Godfrey Davies. Mr. Jones retired about 1955 and Mr. Davies continued. At that time the business was well known for its good bread, cakes etc. which were baked by Mr. Davies on the premises and delivered daily by van over a wide area. By 1968 it became virtually impossible to get bakers willing to work the required unsocial hours so bread was purchased wholesale from a large bakery. Mr. Davies, with the help of his wife still excels in making wedding, christening and birthday cakes to order and small cakes are still available daily in the shop.

WI SCRAPBOOK 1977

The Old Parsonage

This another property identified by name in the manorial record, where it is referred to as 'Gunter's House'.

Joane Thomas inherited this property from her husband Thomas when he died in 1743. She in turn passed it on to her son John, a blacksmith, and his wife Mary, in 1756.

When John died intestate in 1797 the house was occupied by Jane Lloyd a widow. John's only child Elizabeth inherited, she was married to John Hill of Westbury on Trem, Gloucester, a yeoman. They soon sold the house to Anne Thomas, a widow of Woodbrook in Kington. Anne also owned the house to the north of Central Stores.

The property then passed to Anne Thomas's daughter Susannah Bengough in 1826. It was let to her tenants, David Higgins, George Powell, and Samuel Vaughan. Susan Bengough married Edward Woodhouse; she died in 1835 and was buried in Kington.

The houses were left to her daughter Ann, and grand daughter Jane, who married Charles Radcliffe in 1835. They had three children, who should in turn have inherited the property.

At this point there is a break in the record, and after this neither the census of 1841, the tithe nor the Manorial record list any Radcliffes in the parish.

On the tithe map this house is shown as a long building fronting the road, and this and the house to the north of the Stores were owned by John Miller. (The Parsonage was owned jointly with Richard Motley.)

The census would suggest a change from double to single dwelling in the 1860s. After 1880 the house became the residence of the curate. It became part of the Perry-Herrick estate and was let to the Revd S. Montgomery Campbell at the nominal rent of £15 per annum, but estimated to be of the worth £30 per annum. It was bought by Samuel Parry, the station master for £675, and became his residence.

Brook House

This house was built in the 19th century, but there was probably an earlier house on site. The tithe map shows a house extending back from the road side, and judging by the occupations of early residents it might have included a shop.

In the mid 1760s it was occupied by Thomas Hall, a butcher, and his wife Sarah. The 'owner' of the house was listed as Thomas Deykes of the Moor, Eardisley, but it seems likely that Thomas and Sarah, who also owned other property in the parish, had some financial interest in the property. When Thomas Hall died there is an entry by which Deykes secured an alienation of the property from Sarah, in which she transferred title to the property, 'voluntarily and completely' to him. Despite this when Sarah died in 1782 William Deykes, grandson and heir of Thomas, was admitted to the property now occupied by Sarah's son Richard Hall. Deykes and Hall sold the house to Richard Francis, a shopkeeper.

Richard Hall continued to live in the house, and was still there in 1785 and is listed as a 'lender' on the property when it passed to William Lloyd, glover, who lived in Northview.

By the time William Lloyd's son inherited in 1792 the house was uninhabited. (Although Richard Hall did not die until 1801.) William Lloyd the younger moved into the house, and two years later used the property as security on a £40 mortgage from Samuel Price.

Price and Lloyd mortgaged the house further in 1799, for £80 from James Parton of Kington. This mortgage was evidently paid off because in 1805

William and Elizabeth were able to sell the house to William Deykes, a gentleman form Oxenhall, Gloucestershire.

William Deykes died on the 4th March 1827. The property was inherited by his nieces Matilda Rogers and Joanna Harris (daughters of William's brother Thomas Deykes). In August 1837 the Revd John Rogers and Matilda Rogers his wife, and Joanna Harris transferred the property to Thomas Stephens Rogers. This gave the right to use or occupy the property to Rogers, but that Joanna Harris would then take the property upon his death.

Brook House in the Eardisley Sale Catalogue 1918

John Rogers was listed as the owner of the property in 1842, and the house was rented by John Taylor, who used part of it for his shoe making business, with John Watkins and his family occupying the rear of house. The occupants listed in subsequent censuses chart the decline of the property. By 1861 the shop function of the house seems to have gone, and it was rented by labourers.

The inference from the census is that the old house was demolished and replaced in the 1870s. The tenant then was Thomas Palmer, a retired Army Officer and brother to Canon C. S. Palmer.

Thomas Palmer was elected chairman at the first meeting of the Educational Institute in 1876, and continued to support this as chair and later President until he moved from the village in 1910. He was also active in the Foresters.

In the estate sale 'Brook Cottage' was let Mr John Morris, at what was regarded at a low annual rent of £35. He bought the house for £1,300.

Streamside Bungalow

The bungalow by the stream was originally a stable and store for the adjoining paddock, or 'Doctor's Plock'.

Dr Darling later used it as his surgery. It consisted of three small rooms and a garage behind. When he retired in 1935 Dr Darling converted it into a small bungalow.

The Cottage and Jessamine Cottage

The façade is stone work laid in diminishing courses, unusual in the village. The interior is of reclaimed timber which may have come from more than one building. Some of the timber shows evidence of being reused twice. Originally the houses were one room deep; a kitchen outshut was added at a later date.

The site occupied today by The Cottage and Jessamine Cottage was once probably occupied by a single house. In the 1750s the house was owned by William Hayes and his wife Sarah and was occupied by Walter Protherough.

William Hayes was a weaver in Hereford and owner of other properties in the village, including 2–3 Church Road. His wife was a Protherough, and may have been the daughter born in 1724 to William and Sarah. (There are more details of this family given in the description of that house and also Knapp House.)

In 1759 the house passed to Francis Protherough. There is no record of the birth or marriage of Francis in the parish records; he may have been a member of the Hereford branch of the family. The parish records do list the births of their children in Eardisley, Elizabeth born in 1764, William 1766, Ann 1768, Jane 1770, James 1774, John 1776, Thomas 1778, Mary 1781, and Sarah in 1783. Intriguingly Jane was not included in the copyhold of the property until three months before their third child was born. Perhaps Francis was fearful of his health at the time and wanted to make provision for his wife and children.

In 1798 the Protheroughs ran into financial difficulties and mortgaged the house to Richard Pugh a 'gentleman' of Kington for £44.

Francis died in 1806, Jane in 1801 Pugh as mortgagee and William Protherough, their eldest son and now a shoemaker (as his father had been?) living in Upton on Severn, sold the property to Philip Taylor, a miller, of Eardisley for £150. The occupants at the time are listed as John Taylor and David Griffiths. This may be a clue as to when the house was rebuilt as two cottages.

By the time Jane Protherough died all her children would have been old enough to have moved away. The empty house might have presented an opportunity to Pugh to rebuild the house. However this type of redevelopment does not seem to have been the pattern elsewhere in the village, and the houses may simply have been rebuilt after a fire.

In 1817 the occupants were listed as John Fosbury and William Taylor when Philip Taylor sold to Samuel Wright, a gunmaker of Kington, and his wife Elizabeth, for £205. Samuel was listed as the owner by the tithe assessors and the occupants of the two cottages can then be traced separately on the census.

The ownership of the properties after Samuel Wright is difficult to establish but they were both sold into the Perry Estate.

People called Southgate lived in The Cottage; he used to be a saddler and cobbler. "Will you mend these by tomorrow Mr Southgate?" he would reply: "Well I'll see what I can do about it", but you wouldn't get them for a month!

MARY PRICE

Mr Southgate. His wife had died. I remember Ethel, she was the daughter. He sold everything in the way of saddles and stirrups and reins, yes, he sold hunting boots.

JOAN WILLIAMS

I can just remember him, was there another door, it's been filled in but the arch is still there. Mr Southgate would be leaning out of the door and talk to the children as they went to school, an old grey haired man. I used to go there sometimes with my aunt, Edith Brookes, she lived down by the post office, and she and Miss Southgate were great friends.

DOROTHY JOSEPH

Originally from Suffolk, John Southgate and his family were living in Essex before they moved to village in about 1886. He took over the saddler's shop in the village from John Coombe. His wife, Mary Ann, died in 1917.

Their second son, Sydney, was born in the house soon after they moved. He would later work as an apprentice to his father, before leaving home to marry and live in Almeley. In the Great War he joined the 4th Battalion of The King's (Liverpool Regiment), and was killed with 28 of his comrades on Thursday 11 April 1918 when the troop train in which they were travelling crashed. He was 32, and is buried in the Chocques Military Cemetery, Pas de Calais, France.

In the estate sale John Southgate's house was sold to Mr Parry, the railway station master, for £160.

A very pleasing photograph that recently appeared in our local press showing Mr Southgate at work in the saddler's shop at 82 years of age. He is to us all a great example of industry in which he finds pleasure. He still enjoys good health, and comes to Church regularly.

WEOBLEY AND DEANERY PARISH MAGAZINE
MARCH 1935

John Southgate continued to live and work in this house cared for by his daughter Ethel until his death in 1937, aged 83.

Samuel Parry died in 1940 and his sons Samuel and Herbert inherited. William Elliot bought it in 1949; he sold to Elizabeth Comyn in 1956. The house was then bought by the Payne family, who sold it to Eric and Margaret Clarke in 1972.

In 1965 Mrs. Davies of the "The Elms" retired and left the district and the newspaper business was taken over by Mr. Eric Clark who operated from his house at Woodseaves. In 1972 he bought a house in the village and set up "The Cottage Shop" selling newspapers, gifts, sweets etc. from 1972 till 1974 he produced a newspaper for the village called "Chat". This was very popular but very time consuming especially when Mr. Clark had to keep reminding people to bring along all the news items for printing.

From here Mr. Clark also continued with his newspaper round over a very wide area but this year, due to the high cost of transport, he has been forced to cut down the delivery service and now only delivers to the village.

WI SCRAPBOOK 1977

Jessamine Cottage

This cottage was occupied by the same family for almost 100 years. Edward Mason worked as a school master in the village in 1851; he also served as Parish Clark and was an enumerator for the census.

As the children moved away his widow was left in the house alone. Her daughter Lucy was working as a School Governess in Kent in 1881 and she returned to Eardisley to work in the National School in the 1890s.

My uncle and the aunt that brought me up used to go down to Mr Mason and he used to do copper writing and my great aunt, their writing was the same. They used to go, and grandfather paid 2d a week for them go in the evening to learn how to write properly.

LILLIAN BARRON

In honoured memory of Lucy Mason. Who was for 39 years closely involved with this parish, church, day and Sunday schools. This electric light was installed to perpetuate her memory and by reason of her generous benefaction. March 1932.

MEMORIAL PLAQUE, EARDISLEY CHURCH.

Adjoining the Alms Houses was a stone cottage occupied by the District Nurse. Initially this was Nurse Williams, who married the village postman and they eventually had a son Michael. The postman was Wally Davies. Nurse Williams

The Misses Mason.

was succeeded by Nurse Slimming who was a hearty and bonny lady, who somehow managed to ride a bicycle.

BILL BRIERLEY

"Nursing Association.- As we pen these notes, another financial year is concluding. Happily there has not been as elsewhere, severe sickness, nevertheless our Nurse keeps busy tending to the comforts of the chronic, and others, grateful of her help. Meanwhile, the expenses of the Association are unavoidably heavy, and the raising of funds a cause of anxiety. If everyone who could afford it would Support the Nurse by becoming a member, the position would be much easier. Sooner or later everyone has a turn of sickness, and it is a great comfort to feel that we have a resident Nurse. The Whist Drive and Dance on April 12th provided a pleasant evening and added to the fund £5 14s. 7d. We are grateful to the organisers Nurse Slimming and Miss Parsons, and all who gave refreshments and help in other ways."

WEOBLEY RURAL DEANERY PARISH MAGAZINE.
MAY 1934

The Old Cottage (Alms House)

In 1738 Edward Goff was born illegitimate in Huntington, but he moved to London and made his fortune. In his will he left £300 for establishing a school at Hay and an endowment and legacy to the Huntington School. All the rest of his estate was placed in the hands of three Executors in Trust for the Promotion or Establishment of Free Schools in Herefordshire.

The Will was proved in 1815 and almost immediately his executor M. Boyce and a Mr C. West came to Eardisley where they spent upwards of a month setting up a Free School. They rented a house for £10 a year (including taxes). It is thought that this was the house they occupied.

A Mr John Forsbury from Birmingham was appointed as schoolmaster. He was paid quarterly at the rate of £60 a year. The school furniture came to £15 16s 0d and included forms, a desk and a lamp. Stationery for the Eardisley and the Madley Schools came to £35 17s 8d. The teaching was accompanied by preaching, both in Eardisley and around, and with the feeling against Dissenters still strong it is not surprising that in the first year's accounts of the school there are a number of bills for having the windows repaired. The school did not come up to the expectations of the Trustees for whatever reasons and in May 1818 Mr. Forsbury was discharged and the school closed.

The renting of the house ceased in September 1818 and a Sunday School seems to have continued until November 1819 when the Trustees made a payment of £1 10s to a person unknown "for teaching Sunday School." (From an Article by David Gorvett).

It is not clear whether the house continued as a school after this date. In 1841 and 1851 school teachers lived in adjoining properties.

The house became part of the Perry estate and due to its small size was rented to elderly widows. Originally included in the estate sale particulars it was withdrawn and donated to the Parochial Church Council so that:

The Council shall from time to time elect to be inmates of the Curzon Herrick Home such aged or infirm person's, inhabitants of the said Parish of Eardisley as the Council shall consider most deserving of such election. Such inmates may be of either sex and may be either married or single. No able bodied person shall be elected ... it being the intention of the Settlor to provide a home for deserving aged or infirm persons resident in the said Parish

INDENTURE BETWEEN CURZON HERRICK AND THE PCC CONCERNING THE INSTITUTE AND THE WIDOWS' HOME. 14TH DECEMBER, 1923

In 1918 it was occupied by Fanny Chase and Mary Bevan at nominal rents of 1s per annum.

The last tenant Mrs Agnes Powell was given the tenancy in 1963 at a rent of 3/- a week. Mrs Powell paid the rent monthly, giving the church treasurer £1 12s for rent and the other 6/- for the church collection.

In 1973 it became obvious to the neighbours that Mrs. Powell should no longer live alone and so she was transferred to Kingswood Hall and the house became empty. The Council decided that with the advent of the old people's bungalows provided by the District Council there was little need of the home and they decided to sell it. It took three years of negotiations with the Church Commissioners before this was finally agreed to and in 1976 the property was sold to a local builder Mr. Paddy Morgan for £2,500 but after all the various costs had been deducted the Council received £2,146.28. This money was put in the Church Roof Fund.

WI SCRAPBOOK 1965

Next door was the school mistress Miss Mason, and the Alms house that was two cottages. Paddy Morgan turned the place round and put the steps at the back, but before there was a square, you opened the door and the stairs went up in front of you, this was shared, and one lady used one side and one the other.

JOAN WILLIAMS

Birdswood and the Old Police House

Birdswood and the Old Police Station adjoining it to the north may once have formed a single dwelling. Within Birdswood itself are two bays of a cruck-framed medieval hall house that almost certainly had a third bay that would have stood on the old police station site.

Unfortunately, not enough of the framing survives to make more than a tentative analysis of the layout. The northern bay, which formed the single-storey hall, has smoke-blackened roof timbers indicating that there was a central hearth. The south bay was possibly the service end of the building and it is likely that the solar or upper-end accommodation stood to the north where it has been replaced by a cross-wing that now forms part of the Old Police Station.

By the 17th century a first floor had been inserted in the hall and dormer windows added to the roof. The south end wall was also rebuilt in stone, with a large chimney stack and bread oven.

The policeman, Jarrett, lived in the police station. He was great footballer and when he was off duty he used to spend a lot of time talking to Dick Webb the cobbler. He had a grandson that used to live with him by the name of Desmond Jarrett; he had two sons as well. Jarrett was the policeman in the war and before the war.

GLEN PROBERT

Mr Jarrett was the policeman for Eardisley, and I well remember him coming to Eardisley school to warn one of the older pupils that the next time he heard of him smoking he 'would be over that bank', presumably to Court in Kington.

JOHN MORRIS

Another thing they used to do, which they couldn't do now. They could go under the culvert in the village and they would go in at the bottom end and out up along Woodseaves Road and they used to have tins of carbide and cause an explosion, and of course it would sound terrific underneath. The policeman, Mr Jarrett, he used to come out "Now then you boys, what are you up to?" And, of course they would be down this end and he would go up that end and then if they thought he was up that end they would go down this end. Use to have him running up and down quite a bit as they were under there with their carbide.

JOSEPHINE BURGOYNE

Eardisley

The Police Station 1920s

---

7 Church Road

Like the White House, this cottage is also set on a high, stone plinth. It is a timber-framed, two-bay, two-storey house, probably built in the 17th century. The floor appears to have been inserted although it may be the original floor that has been re-positioned following modifications to the roof to increase headroom. There is a large stone chimney stack with bread oven at the south end. This could be a later addition as there is evidence to suggest that it stands on the site of a now lost third bay.

From the 1840s this had bee the home of the Harper family. The last was Lucy Harper, 1863–1951.

You go on up then to Miss Harper, Cottage Shop, who sold haberdashery, a funny old lady, very old she was when I remember her, she sold cottons and bobbins and such like.

JOSEPHINE BURGOYNE

And then the draper's shop, you've heard about Miss Lucy Harper. 'Little girls should be seen and not heard!' The boys used to torment her terribly, they used to have a long rope and tie it on the latch of her door and over to Mr Stephens's door and then knock the doors and run away and one would be opening the door and pulling against the other. Neither of them could open the door, and they thought this was huge fun. Yes, and if you had a doormat outside they thought it great fun to open the door and slide the mat in, that was really something if they could do that! Vandalism today!

JOAN WILLIAMS

Miss Harper. You could go into her and you could buy a pin, and you could buy a hat, you could buy anything. If you wanted a new pair of sheets she'd get them for you. Anything and everything! That little tiny room was absolutely chocker-block – you couldn't pass each other by, it had a big counter

affair with cupboards underneath it and one set of drawers where she kept hats, and she would have a couple perched up on the counter. Dresses, blouses, aprons, men's trousers. You could not pass by. If one came out you had to go back into the room for the other to come out. That's where you went to get news of the village or anywhere else in the surrounding district. She was a nice person I quite liked her, she was very old fashioned, Victorian!

LILLIAN BARRON

Pilgrim Cottage

Described by English Heritage as a probably early 18th century, with mid 20th century alterations and additions, the house is of timber-framed construction with painted brick infill in two bays aligned north/south, with an external rubble chimney with rebuilt detached brick stack at the north end.

Mr Brown, he was a nice man, fatherly. He was a policeman, and he would correct anything that was wrong. This was before the road had pavements on both sides, his

house was the one next to Nicholas' in the village, opposite the post office, Pilgrim Cottage. There was always a policeman in the village. Mr Brown moved to Hay and became a sergeant, quite honestly there wasn't very much for him to do. They used to check animals, swine fever in pigs, and any accidents they had with horses, or cattle getting on the road. But there wasn't much to do, there was no real crime. Everybody was very honest!

LILLIAN BARRON

5 Church Road

This two-bay stone-built cottage probably dates from the late 17th or early 18th century

This house was the village police station, and home of the police sergeant, from the late 1850s to 1895.

Alfred Nicholas and his family lived here in 1918, at an annual rent of £5 4s. It was then bought by Benjamin Povey for £125.

1, 2, 3 and 4 Church Road

These four timber-framed houses have been formed within what was originally a large, medieval hall house. The principal part was a single-storey hall with an open hearth at the centre and, at the south end, a two-storey, three-bay, jettied cross-wing. At the north end there was a two-storey service bay with, what was possibly a secondary hall with a central hearth either for the servants or possibly functioning as a kitchen.

In the 17th century a floor was inserted in the hall and a massive central chimney, with diagonally set stacks, was built to replace the open fire. Alongside the chimney a staircase was introduced. The subdivision to create four separate units possibly took place in the 18th century.

Much of the original timber framing of the building

survives, including the principal arch-braced truss, the spere truss and the joists over the cross passage. The cross-wing has been much altered but the entire roof structure has escaped virtually unchanged.

Tree-ring dating has established that the cross-wing (No. 1) was built using timbers felled in 1434 although the hall range (Nos. 2,3 & 4) has timbers that were felled in the spring of 1513. Clearly, an earlier hall stood on the site of the present range and the evidence of unusually blackened and scorched timbers in that part of the cross-wing roof adjoining the present hall indicates that the earlier structure was most probably destroyed by fire.

Although Thomas and Mary Clarke lived in this house in the late 18th century, the house was called Clark's or Clerk's House in the earliest records. This may refer to an occupant's surname, or indicate that this was the home of a clergyman in the 17th century. It is described as having 'outhouses, three small gardens, court fold and orchard of three Burgages'.

This 'house' today, may have included most or all of the 1–3 Church Road range. The orchard referred to in the description is probably the site of the present day garage. The ownership of this land seems to be linked to this house. For example, at the time of the tithe both were owned by the Revd Rice Price.

Despite the uncertainties over the origin of the name, and even the exact extent of the house, we can be certain that this was a substantial property of some status. In 1743 Henry and Elizabeth Wellington and Henry and Ann Colebatch inherited the house from Thomas Hall, a glover and mercer. Hall had also owned Arboyne House, but while Colebatch lived there for some time, Wellington does not appear to have lived in this property.

By 1745 the house was occupied by William Lloyd, originally from Almeley; he also owned Oakwood.

His son Thomas, a glover, inherited from him in 1757, and he in turn passed it on to one of his sons, Thomas, and his intended wife Mary Winter, in 1786. Before the last sale Richard Francis was renting the house; it was then let to Thomas and Mary Clarke.

Soon after acquiring the property Thomas and Mary married and immediately mortgaged the house to Mary Davies, a spinster, and Elizabeth Price, a widow, for £100.

The mortgage was sold and re-assigned to Mary Davies in 1794, and Charlotte Mainwaring in 1797. In 1799 the mortgage was paid by Samuel Price, shopkeeper, and his wife Bridget and son Samuel.

By 1820 the young Samuel was a farmer, and together with his parents he mortgaged the property to William Taylor, a butcher from Eardisley, for £200.

At this time the property seems to have been occupied as one unit. Sarah Matthews rented the house, and before her a Richard Francis lived there. This changed by 1830 when Joseph Price (son of Samuel Price the farmer) paid the £200 mortgage to William Taylor, before selling the whole to the Revd Rice Price for £300. At the time of the sale the Revd Price is described as occupying part of the property, with William Bufton and William Nott occupying the other parts.

By 1840 the Revd Price had moved to The Rectory and the houses were occupied by agricultural labourers and tradesmen, often with quite large families. During the 1890s Henry Smith opened his butcher's shop at 1, Church Road.

This was taken over by Benjamin Povey:

He bought the four cottages at the bottom [1-4 Church Road], Jack Powell, Rene Townsend, Booth, the Townsend girls, and Jack Davies lived in the end one.

Mr Povey had previously run the Butcher's business taken over by my father and on retirement he acted as an Insurance Agent as a pastime. When he ran the Butcher's business he used the Slaughter-house etc at the premises we later occupied, but conducted his retail business from a wooden shop besides the Grocer's shop. This was later used by Dick Webb the Shoemaker.

BILL BRIERLEY

The dormer of 2 Church Road with iron casement windows

Smith and Son Butchers, 1 Church Road in the early 1900's

Brierley's Butcher's in the 1920s.

The Brierleys started in the 1920s; good, kind, people. They employed local boys, one was Ken Hemmings, from Almeley, for a year. The boys lived in the rooms above the outhouse at the back.

DOROTHY JOSEPH

The Sunday School is still being held – the present teachers are Mrs. Barbara Greenow who lives at "Mowcop" Almeley Road and Mrs. Audrey Sutton who lives in Kinnersley. These two ladies had helped Mr. Bill Brierley who had been one of the mainstays of the chapel for many years. He moved from the village upon his marriage in 1911 and he gave the chapel his piano.

WI SCRAPBOOK 1965

Mr Brierley. He was a very good butcher – Harry always used to say I can tell whose meat it is when he came home from London at the weekend – I can tell this is Brierley's beef and he was always right. They were all pretty good. There were three butchers at one stage in Eardisley.

JOSEPHINE BURGOYNE

– the vestibule they built on the Old House, that was the shop - you can see the coloured slabs in the pavement. There was a gate which was always closed to keep the dogs out, and a door behind. They only used the vestibule and Jack Davies lived there. He became foreman at Deacons of Kington and built the bungalow. Brierley's didn't want the butchers unless they got living accommodation, it was split up and put back to normal house with a butcher's. The butcher boys used to live over the outbuildings.

JOAN WILLIAMS

It is difficult to locate Number 4 Church Road with any certainty in the manorial record. The property described below was to the north of Clark's House, but it might have included other properties.

In 1730 John Crump and Thomas Hall surrendered this house in the possession of William Protherough to Ann Protherough. This may refer to an earlier mortgage. The property had recently been owned by Ann Parlour and rented by John Walker. There is no record of Ann owning other property in the village or when she sold this.

By 1754 John Lewis, a tyler, lived there and William Protherough's daughter Sarah, inherited. Five years later Sarah married William Hayes, a weaver from Hereford, and his name was added to the copyhold. They mortgaged to Walter Williams of Kington in 1760, John Williams was living there.

By 1772 Sarah Protherough had remarried, and the mortgage repaid as she and her husband Samuel Parker sold the house to Thomas and Jane Harris. Henry Beavan was the tenant.

4-5 Church Road was owned by Thomas Jones in 1841. There is no indication of how or when he came by the property.

It was briefly the home of the village constable in the mid 1800s.

Tram Road Cottage

This building was associated with the tramway, and was probably built around 1820 and housed Tram Company employees and later farm workers. It was demolished in the mid 1960s.

The Cottage in the 1930's. (Taken by Group Captain Ellson during his survey of the Tramway)

Gilbert Davies House

On the east side of the main road, just to the south of the millstream there used to be a 'house' which featured in many childhood recollections of the village:

Just beyond were two railway carriages put in place side by side with a wooden structure in between. Mr and Mrs Gilbert Davies and their family lived here and the compartment just inside the door on the side facing the road was used as a tobacco and sweet shop. Their garden went right along to the Mill Brook.

BILL BRIERLEY

Before that bungalow was built that was the orchard that came to the road that all the other bungalows are built on. I think this Gilbert Davies lived in two railway carriages side by side. There was a shop with sweets on the right hand side, and the window pulled up and down on a leather strap. I knew him as Napper Davies. The family had quite a few sons and daughters.

GLEN PROBERT

Do you remember the railway carriages and the sweet shop by the school? Where the bungalow is now, that was the railway carriage, they sold cigarettes and sweets, it was Napper Davies, and the poor man, Charlie. He shook, so we'd go in and if he was there we would have the jar, because he shook more into the bag! Napper got that name from the Knapp House.

DORIS WEALE, EV HATCHER,
DOROTHY JOSEPH, MARY PRICE

Bungalows were built in the 1960s on the orchard in which this building stood.

		Tram Road Cottage	School
1841 CENSUS		No record found.	
	①	Kington Tram Rd Co	
	②	John Lloyd	
1851 CENSUS		Thomas Hatton, 43, Clark to Tram Road Company.	
1861 CENSUS		Sarah Gardner, widow, 54 Elizabeth Gardner, lodger, widow, 50. Thomas Price, widower, 69, Agricultural labourer.	Jessie Lodge, 23, Schoolmaster. Elizabeth Lodge, sister, 27, Schoolmistress. Henry T. Ambler, boarder, 14, Pupil teacher.
1871 CENSUS		James Thomas, 42, Farm Labourer. Mary Thomas, 59. William Ricketts, 20, Labourer. Elizabeth Ricketts, 22.	Jesse Lodge, 33, Schoolmaster. Mary Lodge, 36, Scholar. Eva Lodge, 8; Henry Lodge, 7; Charles Lodge, 6; William Lodge, 4, Scholar Leila Lodge 2; Arthur Lodge, 2m. Eva Browne, Visitor, 10, Scholar Emma Bache, 16, General Servant
1881 CENSUS		David Turner, 33, Farm Labourer. Ann Turner, 33. Thos. Turner, 9; William Turner, 7; George Turner, 6, Scholars. John Turner, 5; Charles Turner, 2; Annie Turner, 1.	William Lock, 25, Schoolmaster Ann Jenkins, widow, 67, House Keeper. Reginald Jenkins, grand son, 10, Scholar.
1891 CENSUS		William Meredith, 38, Agricultural labourer. Mary Ann Meredith, 40. Caroline M. Meredith, 10; William J. E. Meredith, 8; Martha J. Meredith, 2; Minnie E. Meredith, 12, Scholars.	William Lock (absent on day of census) Elizabeth Thomas, Visitor, 22, Dressmaker, Theodora Lock 7; Gertrude M. Lock 6, Scholars. Margaret B. Lock, 10; Kathleen Lock, 2.
1901 CENSUS		Benjamin Gwilliam, 39, Cattleman on farm. Sarah Gwilliam, 34. Rosa Gwilliam, 5; Sarah A. Gwilliam, 4; Arthur G. Gwilliam, 1.	William Lock, 45, National Schoolmaster. Anna M Lock, 49. Gertrude M. Lock, 16; Margaret Lock, 14; Kathleen Lock, 12.
	③		
	④		

① **TITHE OWNER** ② **TITHE TENANT** ③ **1918 SALE**
④ **PURCHASER**

White House

Eardisley House

	White House		Eardisley House east	Eardisley House west
1841 CENSUS	John Cartwright, 45, Agricultural Labourer. Mary Cartwright, 48, Agricultural Labourer. Mary Cartwright, 16, Agricultural Labourer. William Cartwright, 10; Thomas Cartwright, 9. Elizabeth Smyth, 60, Agricultural Labourer. Mary James, 44, Agricultural Labourer.		James Pugh, 35, Stonemason. Hannah Pugh, 40. John Pugh, 40, Agricultural Labourer . Elizabeth Jenkins, 15, Servant.	
	Revd George Coke.		Revd George Coke	
	John Caterick or Cartwright.		James Pugh	
1851 CENSUS	Uninhabited.		John Jenkins, 52, Journeyman Mason. Ann Jenkins, 37. James Jenkins, 16, Mason's labourer. Frances Jenkins, 12; Harriet Jenkins, 11; Eliza Jenkins, 9; Joseph Jenkins, 6, Scholar. Reuben Jenkins, 2; Silvia Jenkins, 7m.	Mary James, 25, seamstress. Mary James, 4. Emily James, 2; Thomas James, 4m.
1861 CENSUS	John Jones, 39, Agricultural labourer. Elizabeth Jones, 5, Scholar.	John Williams, 39, Agricultural labourer. Jane Williams, 34, Laundress. William Price, lodger, 24, Builders labourer.	Thomas Evans, 60, Agricultural labourer. Elizabeth Evans, 57, labourer's wife.	Joseph Bubb, 60, Carpenter. Margaret Bubb, 59. Edward Bubb, 20, Sawyer. Edward Taylor, lodger, 23, General labourer.
1871 CENSUS	John, Jones, 48, Farm labourer. Thomas B. Jones, 40. Mary, Jones, 40, Farm labourers wife. Lodgers: Anna Fleetwood, 56, Charwoman: Edgar Keeble, 37.	John Williams, 45, Farm labourer. Jane Williams, 44, Laundress.	George Bromley, 32, Coachman and Gardener. Elizabeth Bromley, 31. Thomas R Bromley, 5; William Robert Bromley, 2.	Joseph Bubb, 70, Carpenter. Edward Bubb, 30, Sawyer. Martha Bubb, 37. Sarah Williams, Sister in law, 20, General Servant.
1881 CENSUS	John Jones, 57, Farm Labourer. Mary Jones, 48. Thomas Jones, 12, Scholar. William Bubb, Lodger, 9, Scholar.	Jane Williams, widow, 54, Laundress. Mary Jones Price, Niece, 7, Scholar. Samuel Parry, Lodger, 23, Station Master (Railway).	George Bramley, 41, Gardener & Domestic Servant. Elizabeth Bramley, 41. Thomas R. Bramley, 15; William R. Bramley, 12; John Henry Bramley, 9, Scholars.	Joseph Bubb, widower, 80, Carpenter. William Bubb, 36, Gardener. Mary Bubb, 34. Boarders: James Adams, 51; Robert Lavender, 17, Spade Tree Makers Rosa Mary Bubb, Grand daughter, 2m.
1891 CENSUS	John, Jones, 42, Agricultural labourer. Mary Jones, 59. Thomas B. Jones, 21, Agricultural labourer. Boarders: William Bubb, 19, Railway porter; William Hales, 11, Scholar	Jane Williams, Widow, 64, Laundress Elizabeth Price, Niece, 12, Assistant laundress Samuel Parry, Boarder, 32, Railway Station Master	George Bramley, 52, Gardener, Domestic Servant. Ellen Bramley, 46. Thomas Gardener, 39, Waggoner . Mary Ann Gardener, 43. Tracy A Ray, Visitor, 6, Scholar.	
1901 CENSUS	Jane Williams, widow, 74, Laundress, Own account. George Mapp, Boarder, 29, Rural Postman.	Joseph Williams, 33, Waggoner on farm. Elizabeth Williams, 39. George Williams, 11; Walter J. Williams, 8; Margaret A. Williams, 6; Gladys M. Williams, 3.	George Bramley, widower, 62 Groom, domestic.	
	Part of Castle Farm			

Walter Howell's Bungalow

Walter Howells had his wheelwright's, carpenter's shop and saw mills to the west of the main road.

On marrying he built himself and wife a wooden bungalow just beyond the school. He built a large shed across the road and acquired a convertible lorry on which he could put an elaborate glass top to become a hearse or use a coal-lorry body, which Mr Jones, his brother-in-law used for carrying on a coal merchant's business. I can remember the hearse body hanging in the shed long after the lorry had gone out of use. Before the hearse became available coffins had to be taken down the village on a wheeled bier, which had iron bands on its wheels that made a most disturbing noise as it went along followed by a funeral party. Later these iron bands were replaced by rubber bands which greatly improved matters.

BILL BRIERLEY

The Bungalow was demolished in 2004.

The bungalow built by Walter Howells

The School

The school was built in 1857 on land donated by the Perry Estate. A school house was provided for the headteacher on the site

In 1973 when the school house became vacant the trustees knew that this could not be let so they agreed to lease the property to the Local Education Authority for school purposes. In 1999 the house was modernised and upgraded for use as the school office, staffrooms and storage areas.

William Lock and the children of Eardisley School 1880.

The Camp

Things all went haywire in the war and Eardisley became quite an important village, a military camp was built on the back of the Lower Castle Farm, where there was 110 acres of petrol stored, all on ? acre pads, and all in jerry cans. It took them 18 months to haul it in there, and a month to haul it out when D-Day arrived.

After the campsite was emptied of petrol there was a redevelopment programme, and the breaking up of the concrete paths. A lot of it was done by hand and loaded in carts and drawn by horses and delivered to farm sites to repair gateways and lanes that had been neglected during the war years. The camp was then turned into a home for displaced people, who were mainly Poles and Latvians. I can remember the Polish workers; they were extraordinary people to work, they never seemed to tire, and they were always happy to oblige. They were wonderful people.

DENIS LAYTON

Spearman's Timber Yard

Gideon Spearman originally came to Eardisley in 1919 when the Eardisley Estate was sold and bought Cwmma Farm in Brilley of 492 acres, the Wyndham's land below Willersley of 56 acres, and part of Castle Farm, of about 120–130 acres – making him in 1937 the biggest landowner in Eardisley.

He was also a large scale timber merchant, and on the land beside and behind the school he established the Eardisley Steam Saw Mills, which later became the Thames Timber Company and was at one stage the largest, or almost the largest sawmill in the UK. Mr Spearman lived in a corrugated iron bungalow in his timberyard. The timber yard and bungalow can be seen in the aerial view of the village taken in the 1930's (on page v) The bungalow was demolished.

The Thames Timber company, they were a wonderful company because of the volume of the timber they handled and the size of the timber. They also made band saws in Eardisley for cutting the trees which came in as a whole tree trunk from the docks in Liverpool and Bristol. It was brought in on huge lorries and timber carriages. Eardisley had the facility to handle them with big band saws that they made.

DENIS LAYTON

The cottage to the south of the yard was occupied by Mr and Mrs Morgan and their son Frank. Mr Morgan worked for Mr Spearman in the timberyard next door.

When the yard had been taken over by Mr Tauber he built new offices near the road. This later became the doctor's surgery.

Some of the southern part of the timber yard was used for the new fire station in 1965, and in 1993 for the Lady Gardens housing development.

White House

Probably built in the second half of the 17th century, this two-storey, timber-framed house has the main two-bay range set on an east-west axis at right angles to the road with, at the east end, a two-bay cross-wing.

Within the cross-wing is a large chimney stack and bread oven.

A second chimney stack has been built against the west end of the house, possibly on the site of a lost cross-wing.

An unusual feature of the house is that the frame is totally without decoration – even the beams are unchamfered. It is also notable that the timber frame is set on a particularly high, stone plinth.

Significant indications of past use of rooms in the house are the three hop pockets in the floors of the upper rooms. These allowed hop sacks to be suspended during filling and indicate that hop growing was a significant part of the local economy.

This property of a house, garden and two orchards, was sold by John Pugh with Thomas Davies and his wife Elizabeth to the Revd Samuel Hall in 1733.

In 1736 Revd Hall left it to his daughter Ann, now married to another clergyman Samuel Bennet. The assumption must be that they lived in this property; no other tenants are listed, and the neighbouring property owned by Samuel was let.

Samuel added his own poignant comment to an entry in the parish register:

Nov 12 1743.
William s(on) of the Revd. Mr. Saml. Bennet Vicar & Ann his wife bur(ied) to the great grief of his poor father.

In the same register his successor, the Revd Richard Coke, recorded:

Oct 12 1753
The Revd. Samuel Bennet was Buryed he was vicar of this parrish near 18 years he dyed of an Apoplexy fit, in ye forty fourth year of his age & left a disconsolate widow with child, & six children behind him to lament his loss.

This entry disguises the fact that Bennet had died in disgrace. He was a close confederate of Mansell Powell, and a key witness in the subsequent trials. Powell fraudulently obtained the Eardisley estate by forgery, the details of which are in the entry for Castle House. During his appearances in Court Bennet displayed a certain flexibility with the truth, as these extracts show:

Evidence at the Prerogative Court 20th April 1739:

When asked if the Old Gent had made a will, he replied

The White House at the time of the Estate Sale, 1918, divided into two cottages

that he had no will to his knowledge. The only will might be in the hands of Samuel Barnesley in London.

He has looked at exhibit A (Paper writing dated 18th March 1736) knows Old Barnesley's writing as he often received letters from him, and often saw him write in the 5 years he knew him before his death. Never as neatly as in this paper.

Evidence in Chancery 21st September 1747:

Shortly after Old Barnesley's death young Barnesley came to his house and told him he might look upon himself secure as to any fear of a will made by his father. He then told him that Cartwright had shown him writing which he seemed to think was the will.

He had seen Barnesley write signature two or three times, and had received letters from him. He has looked at exhibit A (Paper writing dated 18th March 1736) his best judgement is that it is similar to Old Barnesley's.

When the case eventually went to the Bar of the King's Bench in 1749 the forgery was proved, and Bennet's reputation was ruined.

Ann Bennet mortgaged the house to Richard Coke in 1763; four years later she handed the house over to him. His grandson inherited The White House and Eardisley House in 1832. This house was divided into two cottages and let to farm labourers and their families. By the time of the estate sale it was part of Castle Farm.

Eardisley House

This house was sold by Elizabeth Jones, widow, to John Jones of Staunton on Wye in 1742. She sold the Malt House in the same transaction.

John Jones sold it to the Revd Samuel Bennet and Edward Collins soon afterwards, and Bennet took sole ownership in 1744. The occupant at the time was Blanch Clare.

When Samuel junior inherited from Reverend Bennet in 1760, the occupant was Elizabeth West. Samuel immediately sold the house to Richard Coke of Lower House.

In 1832 Richard Coke's grandson, George Coke, inherited this house and The White House. He still held them at the tithe apportionment, renting this property to James Pugh. The house was split into two units soon after and occupied by two, or even three, families up to the end of the century.

This property is referred to as 'Old Vicarage' in the 1901 census. This is curious, as although it was certainly owned by vicars, no vicar is recorded as living in the property. In the estate sale particulars of 1780 Revd Coke is listed as the tenant in two of his houses.

It was not sold as part of the 1918 sale.

George Bramley lived in the house for over 40 years. In 1876 he attended the Inaugural meeting of the Eardisley Institute, and was elected to the General Council. He continued to serve until 1896.

There was quite a good sized Sunday School. One of the teachers was Miss Money Kyrle who I believe used to live at Eardisley House. Miss Mason was another Sunday school teacher and lessons were usually taken in church.

JOHN MORRIS

Conclusion

This study set out to discover more about the houses of Eardisley and their residents. As a result of the investigation it is possible to draw certain tentative conclusions about the development of the village from the 15th century onwards.

Over thirty of the earlier buildings in Eardisley have been examined. The remains of at least five cruck-framed, open-hall houses have been found, (Cruck House; The Forge; Birdswood; Foxpie Cottage and the south range of Bridge House) and six box-framed hall houses (Lower House; Tram Inn; 1–4 Church Road; The Holme; 10–12 Church Road; and Upper House Farm).

Thus, in total, there are eleven medieval hall houses of varied size and status. With the help of information from tree-ring dating five of these buildings it is possible to state with some confidence that they were all built in the hundred years between 1430 and 1530. In addition one of the barn ranges (5-8 Castle Close); Bank House and probably The Old Forge belong to this period. There may well be others as yet unrecognised.

In contrast to this relatively intense building period there are few houses that can be reliably attributed to the following century (1530 to 1630) other than the hidden, decorative cross wing of Bridge House.

However, there are indications that the mid 17th to early 18th century was a period of revival, with the building of Castle House and its even finer contemporary, near neighbour, Eardisley Park. Indeed, these may have been a catalyst for further new building as evidenced by Hawthorn Cottage; Dairy House; The Nook; The Old House & Woodbine Cottage; Granville and Arboyne House; The White House; Drey Cottage (5 Church Road), Pine Tree Cottage (7 Church Road); Vine House; and the substantial expansion of Upper House Farm at the north end of the village.

These two distinct phases of building do not seem to coincide neatly with known national and regional periods of growth and recession, neither do they conform fully to a theory of the development of the village proposed in an archaeological assessment by the Central Marches Historic Towns Survey in 1996.

The Marches Survey suggested that the earliest settlement in Eardisley centred on the Castle and the Church. To the north of this was a low-lying strip of marshy ground, which the study concluded had always been a meadow. Beyond this was an area of long irregular tenement plots as far as another stream, and then another area of shorter, more regular plots to the north of this. These plots were thought to represent two phases of development of Eardisley as an urban centre in the thirteenth century. This urban phase was thought to have been short lived, and the town was in decline by the end of the medieval period - the 16th century.

Since then an archaeological survey carried out during construction of the Millstream Gardens development found evidence that this area had been occupied from the 12th to the 17th centuries, with at least two buildings on the site. This suggested that the historic core of the village extended further to the north than the Marches Survey supposed, and that the return of this plot to agriculture was evidence that the village was in decline by the seventeenth century.

The present study has shown that widespread development occurred within the tenement plots in the 15th century. It is not clear whether this represents building on plots laid out and not used, or comprehensive redevelopment, (after destruction by Owain Glyndwr?) The observation by the Marches Survey of the hall as the typical medieval house form in the village is confirmed.

The reason for this development is not known, but the influence of the Lord of the Manor would have been pivotal in this period of growth. In the light of these findings a re-evaluation of the role of the Baskervilles should be made, in particular the four generations represented by John (1407/08–1455), James (about 1430–1485), Walter (about 1456–1508) and James Baskerville (1494–1546).

The findings of this study confirm the view that the market place was originally wider and that market encroachment has taken place on the west side but not the east. It is clear that the earlier (15th century) triangular market area was defined by a line drawn from the front of the Tram Inn, south across the front of The Forge, to meet the west corner of Bridge House rather than the east as at present. Thus, the entire decorated side of the Bridge House cross wing would have been visible from the north end of the market. It is probable that the front gardens and especially Arboyne House represent 17th century encroachment. It may be that the front gardens of the houses along the north side of the market area are also encroachment – possibly by consent if there was a declining need for market space.

Further research is needed to find if the loss of the market square was related to a loss of trade, or whether this was simply an adjustment to a different form of trading within houses.

The second period of housing development in the mid 17th to early 18th century coincides with the tenure of William Barnesley as Lord of the Manor. Very little is known about him, and the possibility that he made a significant contribution to the village has been overshadowed by the scandal over the inheritance of his estate.

From the analysis of the Manorial records we now have a clearer picture of the ownership of the buildings in the 18th century. Many of the houses were owned by families closely tied to the village, often tradesmen or minor gentry. Many of the houses were passed down through inheritance through a number of generations. The impression gained is that the sale and transfer of property in this period is related more to changes in individual circumstances that more general factors. Further research is required to confirm this.

The Marches Survey noted the lack of any significant building between the mid 18th to the late 19th centuries, and cite this as evidence of stagnation in this period. This study suggests that the reality might be more complex. There was a lack of housing development during this period, but the population of the village was not in decline, it was growing. The census for 1841 records 768 people in the parish in 175 households. By 1871 this had risen to 902 in 223 households. The census tables show that these extra people were accommodated within the existing houses. Much of this population growth could be related to the development of the railway. Despite the growth in population there does seem to have been decline in the wealth in the village, shown by the number of properties acquired by the Perry-Herrick estate in the latter half of the century.

This study has not cast any light on the position of the early settlement. The Central Marches Survey identified three 'tenement plots' as possible sites for the early settlement. These are now occupied by Castle Barns to the north west; the Rectory to the south west; and the School, White House, and Eardisley House to the south east. However there is no evidence that these areas are Medieval. Indeed, as the boundaries of two of them are formed by the line of the Tramway, and part of one boundary is not marked on the tithe map, we can say with some certainty that they are not.

The area to the north east (Orchard Gardens) was not included as part of the settlement. This seems a major omission. The ground level of this area matches the Church and Castle Barns; all are raised above the road. The Tithe map of 1841 suggests that the road to the east continued as a track, with the road to the Castle this would have formed a significant crossroads near the Church, and the focus for the village.

Nor has this study found any evidence of when the tenement plots in the current village were laid out. The question of why the form of the plots should be so different in the centre and north of the village, and which were developed first is also unanswered. Further research to systematically measure the tenement plots and survey the area surrounding the Castle and Church, might provide useful information on the early development of the village.

Local history was once defined as the study of the 'origin, growth, decline and fall of a local community', and to some extent this study comes within that definition. But we hope that it is also more than that and, that as well as the wider picture, we have glimpsed the lives of some of the ordinary and extraordinary people of this village.

Appendix

The Sources of Information

Documentary Sources

The survival of documentary evidence throughout Herefordshire is rather uneven. Many of the records of county wide events such as visitations or collections survive, as do the records of some of the larger families, but the survival of the uniquely local often depends on nothing less than chance. Much of this information is held by the Herefordshire Archive Office, but there must be many more documents in private hands. This is a concern, not only because these are not available for research, but because they are not being stored in ideal conditions and are liable to be lost.

Where documents have survived they often describe one incident, or events in the life of one family. They fail to give us a wider picture of the whole village or show how things changed over time. To map out the lives of the ordinary villagers who have shaped and formed the community requires using many sources.

Manorial Records

The scarcity of labour following the Black Death in the 14th century meant that the feudal obligation of villein tenure to provide certain services to the lord of the manor had to be commuted to money payments. This led to the creation of tenancies in which land was held by right of title entered into the manor court roll, and tenants were provided with a copy of that entry – hence *copyhold*. When transferring property the copyhold tenant surrendered it to the lord of the manor who then granted it to the new tenant who paid a fine, usually one year's manorial rent. Copyhold was abolished in 1922.

The manorial records for Eardisley are in ten books and cover the period 1635 to 1926. They are in private hands, and are not readily available. However the late Mrs Margaret Hall made detailed notes of the entries from about 1700. The notes are reasonably complete after 1720 and record about 800 property transactions in the parish in these years.

These records offer a mass of useful information, but they do have certain limitations. Property is rarely named, it is described by the court in relation to the surrounding properties, and these change over time. Simply identifying a property and building up a sequence of owners can be difficult. There is a lack of consistency in the record. Some records use the names of neighbouring land owners, others use the names of neighbouring tenants, or a combination of the two. Some properties are always identified by the original pattern of neighbours in the 1700s, in others the pattern changes as the neighbours change, and yet others do not include any information to identify the property at all. The manorial record refers to a plot of land. The fact that houses have been demolished and rebuilt is very rarely recorded.

Using the names of the vendor and purchaser and details of surrounding properties it has been possible to reconstruct the history of many properties. To ensure consistency in the interpretation of these records they have only been accepted when they could be verified against corroborating details in the tithe, census or parish register of births, marriages and deaths.

Freehold Title Deeds

Copyhold was one form of property holding, the other was freehold. This is the holding of property in absolute possession, and it was not subject to manorial custom. There are several properties in the village which have historically been freehold, and some of them have full sets of deeds, and these deeds created by a transfer of ownership often 'recite' previous transfers. However many deeds in the village only go as far back as the estate sale in 1918. Earlier deeds have been lost in the records of the Herrick family, a few are stored in Leicestershire Record Office.

Tithes

A tithe is usually a tax of one tenth of the annual produce of land or labour to support the clergy and the church. The Tithe Commutation Act of 1836 allowed tithes to be commuted to rent charges, and commissioners were appointed to each parish to negotiate land values. The maps and apportionment books completed in about 1840 created a unique record, allowing individual parcels of land and their owners and tenants to be identified.

Census

The first census of population in England and Wales was held in 1801 to provide population statistics. Most of the records between 1801 and 1831 did not record details of individuals. However from 1841 more information has been gathered. The census is made every 10 years, and individual details are available for public inspection after 100 years, so the latest available at present is 1901.

Using the census for research is not without problems. Although larger houses are usually identified, all the enumerators in Eardisley have been very reluctant to identify properties. This is understandable perhaps where, as today, property was identified by the name of is owner. It has been possible to identify the residents in each house by cross referencing with the tithe and manorial records.

The census records rely on the honesty, or the memory, of individuals. There are several examples of names, ages and places of birth changing between censuses. Where residents were illiterate the enumerator often wrote down what he heard, or thought he heard, on the form. This can lead to some interesting spelling and variation in names, for example Protherough, Protheroe, and Prothero to describe the same family. This problem also occurs within the parish register. Throughout we have retained the original spelling or details found in the sources.

Maps

Few early maps of the parish exist. Estate maps were prepared in the late 1700s but only two fragments are known to survive. One of the Perry estate shows Parton Farm, while the other of the Foley estate shows Bollingham. No maps of the village survive from this period. The Ordnance Survey mapped the village at one inch to the mile in 1833, more detailed maps were not available until the 1890's. There may be other maps which have been kept privately. One such map was of the sewerage system in 1900 which was retained by the parish clerk, Mr William Cartwright, and is now in the Hereford Record Office. This map also records the names of residents, and was invaluable in checking the census lists.

Photographs

Photographs and old postcards provide details of the ownership of shops and businesses and the appearance of the village. A large collection of photographs collected by David Gorvett has been lodged in the Hereford Record Office.

Parish Registers

The register records all the births, marriages and deaths in Eardisley from 1633.

Wills and Inventories

Wills and inventories are public documents, and are therefore readily available. However relatively few people made wills, and there seem to be many property owners in the village who did not.

Tax

A land tax was levied between 1692 and 1832, and records exist for Eardisley between 1783 and 1830. These documents list the owners and tenant of a property and its valuation. The location of most of the properties is not given, but these have been useful in confirming relationships between landlord and tenant.

Pictures